Advanced
CAREER
STRATEGIES
FOR WOMEN

Advanced
CAREER
STRATEGIES
FOR WOMEN

How To Make It To
The Top Faster

Marilyn Machlowitz

CAREERTRACK PUBLICATIONS / BOULDER, COLORADO

Book and Cover Design: Bobbi Benson
Composition/Graphic Artist: Cheryl Warner
Cover Photo: Willie Gibson

Type: California Roman
Library of Congress Catalog Card Number: 84-71203
Printed First Edition in the United States of America
ISBN: 0-943066-20-4

Dedicated to my brother, Dave

Table Of Contents

Part IV: Successful Strategies for Overcoming Obstacles

Part V: The Last Word

Acknowledgments

Many people have exerted a profound influence on my thinking about careers, in general, and women's careers, in particular. My parents, Roy and Eleanore Machlowitz, gave me the privilege of growing up in a two-career household long before it was fashionable. My grandmother, Ida Levin, regaled me with stories of sewing in sweatshops on Fifth Avenue at the start of this century. When my consulting work takes me to elegant executive suites on that same street, I think about the progress achieved.

Thanks are due, too, to the editors of *Working Woman, Family Circle* and *Ladies' Home Journal.* Most of the material in this book originally appeared in those magazines, and I appreciate their kind permission to reprint my articles here. Additional publishers, editors and writers have provided me with the opportunity to puzzle over, ponder and see published my thoughts on business and behavior. I thank them all, but especially Martin Edelston, Adam Meyerson, David Asman, T. George Harris, Joann Lublin, Georgia Dullea, Enid Nemy, Joan Motyka, Linda Small, Megan Murray, Jo-Ann Wasserman, Ellen Kolton, Bob Luce, Marty Lasden, Judy Linscott, Hugh Vickery, Susan McHenry and Didi Moore.

My terrific lecture agents—especially Blanche Ross and Dee Ann Mernit of Ross Associates in New York—have provided me the opportunity to meet with, and work with, large groups of executives of both sexes from Palm Beach to Palm Springs.

I am lucky enough to number among my corporate clients, my colleagues, and my friends a number of influential and inspiring leaders. My thanks to all of them, but especially Peter Drucker, Daniel Yankelovich, Madelyn Jennings, Ellen Golden, Monita Buchwald, Judy Blatman, Robert Half, Charni Rosenberg, Faye Crosby, Rosabeth Moss Kanter, Martin Greller, Carol Schreiber, Carol Galligan, Ethel Spector Person, Cynthia Fuchs Epstein, Jan Barkas, Amitai Etzioni, Robert Lee, Linda

Jones, Harold Pincus, Larry Newman, Eden Collinsworth, Bruce Yaffe, Alice Young, Rosalie Wolf, Ellen Poler, Carter Hopkins, J. Richard Hackman, Daniel Levinson, Virginia Schein, Edgar Schein, John van Maanen, Marcia Fox, Bartlett Cocke, Lanny Harer, Lanny Jones, John Connorton and Sol Warhaftig.

Hundreds of experts and executives graciously agreed to sit still for interviews and I am grateful to them.

Then, too, there are those in my firm—notably Tova Reiner —those at Cloverdale Press and those at CareerTrack—especially Jeff Salzman, James Calano, Pam Schroer and Delynn Copley —who have been delightful additions to this woman's career.

Marilyn Machlowitz
New York City
March 1984

x

Author's Note

You will notice that this volume presents information relevant to your personal life as well as to your professional life. There are a couple of reasons for this. My expertise—my Ph.D. is in organizational psychology—and my experience—as a management consultant—convince me that lives are not as compartmentalized as the sections of the average library. Some issues and events—getting promoted or getting married—will have implications for all aspects of your life.

With the exception of the introduction and the conclusion, all of the chapters were published in *Working Woman, Family Circle* or *Ladies' Home Journal.* Some of the titles for people mentioned in these pieces may have changed and, indeed, some of the women mentioned may have gone on from one employer to another. This is a highly mobile group!

I recommend reading the whole book through and then retaining it for easy reference—for dipping and delving into particular sections later. Some of the material may merely be "nice to know" now. Later, it may move into the "need to know" category for you.

Questions about careers are so commonplace today that you would be the exception and not the rule if you didn't have any. This book provides the same insight and inside information I shared with my career counseling clients until corporate consulting took over my practice. If you want to get in touch with a reputable career counselor in your community, I recommend writing to Catalyst, 14 East 60th Street, New York, NY 10022.

If you want to get in touch with me to offer suggestions for any subsequent editions, please write c/o Post Office Box 387, New York, NY 10156.

Books by Marilyn Machlowitz

WHIZ KIDS

WORKAHOLICS

ADVANCED CAREER STRATEGIES
FOR WOMEN

Advanced
CAREER
STRATEGIES
FOR WOMEN

PART ONE

Getting Going
And Growing

1 | INTRODUCTION: WOMEN TODAY: PERSONAL AND PROFESSIONAL TRANSITIONS

Today's emphasis on "having it all" obscures the fact that each of us defines "all" differently. There are those, for instance, for whom no winter is complete without a stint on a sandy beach. Then there are others who never set foot in the Caribbean, but crave Colorado's ski slopes. There are those who find a second home a relaxing retreat and others for whom it is only a big bother. There are executives who yearn to break out of the "broil or boil" cooking routine their busy weekdays dictate (and would love to cook up a storm) whereas others find even broiling and boiling excessive.

A recent panel discussion in Manhattan elucidated these, and other, issues of importance to today's women. That such exchanges have been elevated from private phone conversations to public forums is significant in itself. This is the first generation of young women exhorted to "trade off" instead of "give up" one option or another.

But this privilege brings its own set of pressures. While it was once believed that management and marriage or motherhood were incompatible, it is now implicit that it is mandatory to combine them. A woman's life is thought to be somehow lacking if all three elements are not present at once.

Recent psychological research adds new impetus to this imperative. No longer are multiple roles said to be a recipe for overwork and overload. Rather, according to the authors of *Relative Deprivation and Working Women* (Oxford University Press) and *Lifeprints* (McGraw-Hill), multiple roles protect the women who hold them. The analogy the researchers offer is

3

that of not putting all your eggs in one basket or of diversifying your investments.

Yet, just as not every woman wants to be an executive, not every woman wants to be either a wife, a mother or both. What does seem clear, however, is that no woman wants to have any of these options taken from her.

However, keeping one's options open inevitably closes a few. While the panelists, of whom I was one, carefully eschewed the word "sacrifice," members of the audience were quick to mention it. Sacrifice, it seems to me, is the term we use for those outcomes we don't get to choose—and would not choose, if we could. Our preference, of course, is for "choices."

Such semantics bespeak our need not for choice, but for control. But control over life's course is, at best, illusory and often elusive. Which term might apply, for example, to those unbidden consequences of freely-taken actions?

Then, too, people may seek control over some aspects of life when they lack it—or lose it—in other areas. The recent economic uncertainties that led to large-scale white-collar layoffs led many managerial and professional employees to abandon the notion that they could control, or even predict, the shape of their careers. Some, according to a Detroit psychiatrist, sought to compensate by controlling their health through joining health clubs or jogging.

Then, too, even satisfying all of one's options at once can impose other threats. Over two decades ago, sociologists identified the "life crunch" created by trying to establish a career and a family simultaneously. Their subjects, then, were mostly men, but the same can hold true for women.

Lurking beneath the debates about simultaneous vs. sequential life activities is a lingering set of societal timetables. These seem to suggest that there is a "perfect" time—or at least a right time—to accomplish certain goals.

The wholesale acceptance of such beliefs leads to, among other things, the existence of "now or never" thinking. I have had a series of female assistants between the ages of 20 and 23. Each of them—even in the '80s—has appeared to go through a bout of nervousness when the first flurry of her college friends began to marry. They worried, I surmise, that they had missed what might be their "last chance." I submit that this mind-set is present at other points, as well. The rash of relationships that blossom just prior to graduation from law school or business school that culminate in rushed—if conveniently-timed—June weddings suggests a variant of the same fear.

Such temporal prescriptions also impute permanence to those decisions that are, in fact, changeable. The prevalence of divorce, first children at forty and second careers at fifty proves that some decisions are not irreversible.

Just as the preceding "either-or" thinking created some animosity between women who worked outside their homes and those who did not, the existence of and insistence on "having it all" is causing enmity between women who have children and those who do not. A close friend of mine, who has not yet had—and may not have—children, even resents the publicity given groups with such names as "Mothers For Peace," for the pro-parent prejudice such nomenclature seems to imply. Another friend reports that her co-workers seemed to rejoice at the news of her pregnancy, but tended to give her the cold shoulder when she returned from maternity leave and had clearly joined the other "camp." Still another woman pursues a demanding career while her sister stays home to rear children. Each of them prefaces any discussion of the first woman's work with the caveat, "But, of course, I/you couldn't do this with children"—a sentiment which neither of them knows to be true, but one which both prefer to believe is gospel.

Furthermore, my own career consultations with individual clients lead me to conclude that many of the musings about the "road not taken" have less to do with its satisfactions than the dissatisfactions of the path pursued. For instance, a lot of the switches from office to home that working mothers may be making (or, at least, the media are making much of) occur six to ten years into a career when one has to begin to come to terms with what one has—and has not—attained. Potential and the premise of unlimited promise are no longer enough, and a lot of women—and men—start sounding a lot like Peggy Lee, as they wonder, "Is that all there is?"

Managers should also avoid the natural envy directed toward those who can carry off more than they themselves can. We don't all possess the same amount of energy, require the same amount of sleep or devote equal amounts of attention to avocational pursuits. The intolerance that can be directed toward those tackling more than we ourselves do reflects and reveals a sense of our own inadequacy. So, instead of attacking those who "have it all," or hope to, perhaps we should merely make sure that we are going after—and, one hopes, getting—that which we ourselves want.

Twenty years ago, The Invisible Woman was a popular educational toy. She was a transparent plastic statue that provided children with an internal anatomy lesson. Today, while women are more active in public life, in private life, we are still treated as though our public, professional personas are invisible.

Unless we are dealing with someone who is aware of our professional roles, all too often the assumption is still that we don't have such identities. All of us, of course, have more than one identity, but our female role often overshadows all others, at least in other people's eyes. Our customary workday identities seem to do a disappearing act whenever we move out from behind our desks or work stations.

For instance, a friend of mine heads her own nine-person firm. For a while, her most senior associate was a man of her age. When they walked into meetings, she recalls, it was automatically assumed that he was her boss. Similarly, I once took a date to a dinner-dance given by a company that is a client of mine. All evening, the others at our table asked my friend how he knew our host. And, all evening, he had to respond, "I don't—she does."

Even on those occasions when our work identities are acknowledged, they may be treated as subordinate to our gender identities. In conversations with relatives or friends, a woman's commitment to her career may be down-played or put down. Many women have crowed about a promotion or another coup, only to hear, "That's nice, dear, but when are you going to start a family?" Another woman I know has Sunday supper with her in-laws. Every week, she and her husband are shooed-out early so, as her mother-in-law explains, "Bob can get to his office the next morning." It is never mentioned that the woman in question also has to get to *her* office the next morning, or that she happens to be due there an hour earlier than Bob is due at his.

What's At Stake

It is easy to dismiss such women's sensitivity to these slights as insecure griping, but there are larger issues at stake. These automatic assumptions show that sex-role stereotypes are alive and well. Any working woman over twenty-five has done battle against beliefs that she attended medical school to meet a doctor, that she was "too pretty" to be an engineer, that if she said she taught, she meant kindergarten and not college, and the like. When you think the "war" is over—and you're too tired to fight any more battles after hours—demeaning, demoting comments can feel as though they are slaps in the face.

All that is at stake, then, is our sense of ourselves. If we choose to divest ourselves of a professional identity, it should be our choice to do so. It is not up to others to discern or determine which of our identities is the most important. Our priorities are our own. Now that they no longer need to be societally-set, we are entitled to be offended when it appears they still are.

What To Do

• *Make sure you are clear about your chosen identities.*

When you are uncertain, you may either signal this to others or simply be more alert to signals from them. Avoid giving others the opportunity to dismiss what you do. If you describe yourself as *"just* a secretary" or *"only* a financial analyst," others may feel free to deprecate what you do, too. Try to close the gap between who you are and what you do. If you distance yourself from your full-time job as a copywriter by maintaining that you are *"really* a playwright," others may devalue your paying career, too.

• *Seize the limelight for yourself.* Certain jobs require that you leave the limelight to others. There are public relations specialists whose words appear in the newspaper everyday but whose names never do. There are editors who rewrite books only to watch authors receive the rave reviews and the royalty checks. You might benefit from obtaining more direct recognition than your work permits. The PR person or the editor, might want to tack on a sideline—for instance, freelance writing—that requires less anonymity.

In other fields, it is worth wondering whether it truly is necessary for you to stay on the sidelines quite so much as you do. I have counseled women who seem to favor the role of perpetual protégée. Like Avis, they tend to be Number Two—even when they need not be. If you have always positioned yourself as the aide or assistant to a prominent powerhouse, perhaps it is time to take a job where you can be the star.

Introduce your other identities in conversations after five. If you're at the kind of cocktail party where you lose your last name as well as your first and are introduced as "Al's date," "Harold's wife," or "the woman with whom Charles lives," interject a funny anecdote from your day. Or tell a story that reveals some details about what it is you do for a living. You can make your point easily this way without having to sound strident.

• *Understand the dynamics of personal relationships.* The "friend" who chooses to ignore your career successes and to focus on your personal inadequacies—the five pounds you said you'd lose and haven't, the haircut you needed last week— may, of course, feel inferior to you in the professional sphere. By "forgetting" about that, she can shift the seesaw so that she winds up on top.

The relative who treats management as though it is your avocation and motherhood as though it is the only vocation, may simply subscribe to a different set of values than you do. She, however, may be questioning her priorities and be threatened by yours. So she may try to comfort herself by confronting you.

• *Examine the circumstances underlying your constellation of identities.* Like many multi-faceted women, I get a lot of grief from people who cannot seem to understand that it is quite possible for me to be a consultant as well as a writer. My conclusion, I'm sorry to say, is that those who are unsure as to whether they possess any abilities at all tend to be envious of those who appear to possess two talents or more.

Sometimes, the gap between different roles is simply too great. If life on the road is replete with pompano en papillote and dinner at home consists of dunking a plastic pouch of frozen food in boiling water, you may want to put more care and even "glamour" into your home life. When the Chairman of the Board feels it is a demotion to become "a 'mere' member of the family" when she opens the front door, her home life can be headed for a hard time.

• *Hang on to your numerous roles.* Don't think you have to give up any of them—or all of them. Recent research at Wellesley College and Yale University shows that multiple identities protect women and enhance their happiness. This isn't to suggest that there won't be moments when you grow confused by or conflicted about your various roles. This is just to say that on multiple choice tests you do have to choose one answer. In real life you don't.

2 | CAREER MYTHS

As a career counselor, I have to debunk a lot of mistaken beliefs about careers. Ten of the most common myths and the corresponding facts are given below. Don't be surprised if the way things really work contradicts your view of the way things are *supposed* to work. The rules of the game change so fast that almost everyone has some catching up to do.

Myth: You have to have a five-year plan

It is good to have goals, so long as they are flexible and you update them regularly. As one high-ranking woman executive told me, "You may change over time. Business changes; the economy changes. To adopt a single way to get what you want is limiting."

In careers, unlike geometry, the shortest distance between two points is not always a straight line. Careers may take more indirect routes, and seeming detours may turn out to be the best path. One woman left a staff position to join another company where her specialty permitted her to assume a line job. She then joined a third organization in a high-level staff job that would not have been open to her had she skipped the intermediate line position.

Myth: You must stay in a job for at least two years

There is no magic number of years to stay in one job to make your résumé look good. Much of the stigma associated with job-hopping has disappeared; it may, in fact, be good for your career. If you find that a new job is not right for you, start your job search immediately. The best time to change jobs is before you *have* to do so. If you wait too long, your dissatisfaction will affect your performance. When you don't feel proud of your accomplishments, it is hard to present yourself well to a prospective employer.

There are other dangers to staying put too long. If recruiters and interviewers sense how miserable you are, they may shy away or offer you a lower starting salary than they might if you were in a stronger bargaining position. Then, too, you may succumb to what I dub the "silver platter offer." This is an offer that you would not consider under better circumstances but accept out of desperation just because it is handed to you. Managers who accept such offers usually discover that they have jumped from the frying pan into the fire.

Women are far more likely to stay in a place too long than they are to jump around. If, for instance, you started as an administrative assistant but managed to move up the ladder, you may fail to receive the recognition that is your due because your co-workers' perceptions are slow to shift. You probably will find it easier to establish your authority elsewhere. Then, too, if you haven't changed positions, you may find that your ten years of experience really boil down to one year's experience, repeated ten times.

Myth: You need one more credential or job experience before making a move

Women, in particular, want to overequip themselves and acquire too many credentials. They decide to wait until they have five more presentations or an MBA under their belts before moving upward. One woman I know has stayed in the same job for several years because she has yet to master national marketing for her firm. Because she has handled local and regional marketing for her large company, moving to a smaller firm to manage national marketing might be less of a leap than she thinks.

Delaying tactics often mask fears about assuming new responsibilities. Remember that companies wouldn't offer on-the-job training programs if they expected everyone to jump into new jobs equipped with all the requisite skills. Insecurity and self-doubt make women susceptible to academic come-ons. The Katharine Gibbs schools, for instance, used to advertise that "the more you learn, the more you earn." This is a noble sentiment but one that almost any Ph.D. can tell you is not true. In fact, sociologist Ivar Berg, Ph.D., calls this fallacy "the great training robbery."

Before going back to school, try to transfer the talents you already possess to a new job or to an expanded version of your current job. If you want to become a neurosurgeon, you must go to medical school, of course. But you can make other transitions without additional education. Ideally, a new job should permit you to draw on the skills you already have, as well as encourage you to develop new ones.

Myth: Being homebound will hold you back

Careers don't disappear, particularly if you have been working for a number of years. One professor I know was afraid that a glaring gap on her record would do her in when she applied for a prestigious grant. Indeed, her fears seemed warranted when the federal funding agency sent her a form letter asking her to account for those eight years. Worriedly, she replied that she had been a homemaker then, and kissed good-bye all hopes of getting the grant. When it was awarded and firmly in hand, she inquired about that alarming form letter. It was, she learned, a routine request to find out whether she had been trying to hide a prison term.

Don't drop out of sight if you happen to be homebound temporarily because of a bad back or a new baby. "The longer you'll be away, the more routinized your contact (with former employees, co-workers and your boss) needs to be. Regular phone calls or appearances condition your colleagues to hear from you at set intervals," write Meg Wheatley and Marcie Schorr Hirsch in their book *Managing Your Maternity Leave* (Houghton Mifflin).

Informal contacts can be useful, too. One psychologist attends her professional society's monthly meetings although she is not working at present. Another woman chooses volunteer activities that are relevant to her field, banking. Instead of baking for her church's cake sale, for example, she prepares the church budget. While these women's careers will progress more slowly, they won't be stalled.

Myth: You can escape office politics

Many women think that using their personal connections or playing office politics constitutes cheating. Hardly. Political maneuvering can determine who gets ahead and who stands still. A man who has moved up rapidly within his publishing organization traces his ascent, in part, to an incident earlier in his career. He happened to learn that his company's head was a golf enthusiast. From then on, he checked with the president's assistant about his upcoming travel destinations and always passed on articles about great golf courses the man could visit. So revamp your mental job description to include political awareness and maneuvering as part of your work, not an intrusion.

Myth: It is easy to work with people

Many of the women who seek my advice tell me right away that they want to work with people. Their unspoken assumption is that working with people will be more fun and less frustrating than working with papers or machines. In fact, working with people is hard.

Technicians, specialists and professionals who are promoted to managerial posts find that it takes months or years to master such difficult tasks as delegation and discipline. Many dread grappling with performance appraisals. Others find that they miss the relative autonomy of their previous positions (see "Corporate Passages," page 32).

Senior executives frequently wish that they had paid more attention to such "soft" fields as organizational behavior when they were in business school, instead of concentrating on such "hard" specialties as operations research. Popular wisdom has it that there are no problem people, only people problems. But there are moments when top executives are tempted to disagree.

Myth: A lot of jobs are glamorous

Every job has its drawbacks. As one consultant to the United Nations says: "Ninety percent of every job is floor-scrubbing." Even Diane Sawyer, the anchorwoman of the "CBS Morning News," has to turn down exciting dinner engagements to go to bed early so that she will be awake for her show. The presidents of prestigious universities sometimes say that they feel as though they are little more than fund raisers as they gad about to alumni groups. And a statistical analyst, who enjoys status and prestige outside her retail organization, has confided to me that her job really consists of routine "clerk work": rearranging numbers on charts and graphs.

Myth: You must have a mentor

Few people actually have mentors. In my recent study of 60 men and women who achieved success at an early age, only two reported the aid of a mentor. In *The Woman in Management* (ILR Press), Rosabeth Moss Kanter, Ph.D., recommends instead that you seek sponsors: persons who can provide more specific and time-limited assistance than mentors. In conference presentations and journal articles, Kathy Kram, Ph.D., suggests turning to your manager for many of the functions a mentor fulfills—introducing you to influential people and including you in meetings. And your co-workers and friends can fulfill some of the other roles of a mentor—serving as a sounding board, for example.

Myth: You must be able to move when your company wants you to

For a long time, it was assumed that upward-bound women managers were at a disadvantage because of the requirement to relocate. But the rise in the numbers of dual-career families and of men who are reluctant to move, as well as soaring moving and mortgage costs, mean that many companies are reconsidering their relocation policies.

In the 1950s, IBM was said to stand not only for International Business Machines, but also for "I've Been Moved." Today, though, an IBM spokesman says that "we have people who joined IBM at one location and still are at that location many years later. Our relocation rate has declined from 5 percent of the working population in the mid-1970s to 3 percent in the '80s. We now say that it's not necessary to relocate to have a successful career, although, of course, relocation does enhance career opportunities."

Myth: Your boss will look after your interests

A woman at a large financial institution tells the story of a boss who promised her a promotion and described it in such glowing terms that a bystander might have thought he was nominating her for a senior vice-presidency. All he actually was offering her was the possibility of moving from salary level 13 to salary level 14. She, wisely, got him to give her a realistic job preview and then looked outside her company for opportunities to advance.

The power of many superiors to promote their staff's interests is restricted by salary ceilings, hiring freezes and promotion slow-downs. Despite corporate attention to career development, your advancement is still your own responsibility. You can't count on anyone else to take care of it for you.

PART TWO

Mystiques That Are Mistakes

3| STILL ROOM AT THE TOP

Too many women have moved too far, too fast, some observers claim. Yet current research shows that relatively few women have reached the ranks of *senior* management. Why, despite women's presence in the "pipeline" leading to the top jobs, have so few pushed—or been pulled—through? What are the obstacles blocking the way? Recent research shows both support for, and surprises about, some of the most commonly held reasons for women's underrepresentation at the top.

Mariann Jelinek, Ph.D., of McGill University's Faculty of Management, and Anne Harlan, Ph.D., of Wellesley College's Center for Research on Women, suggest that women set their sights too low. Seven percent of the male MBA students in their study sample expected their starting salaries to exceed $65,000; not one woman did. Twenty-eight percent of the men thought that their salaries eventually would top $200,000 whereas only nine percent of the female management students did. Whether these lower aspirations reflect pessimism or merely realism, Jelinek and Harlan maintain that goal setting is essential both to effective managing and to getting ahead.

Getting The Skills

Women also may limit their mobility because they lack certain skills. Public speaking, for example, provides a boost up the ladder—and becomes mandatory once you've arrived. While fear of public speaking is widespread, phobia about it is especially pronounced among women. Another hindrance is the avoidance of computers and other complex equipment. While "math anxiety" holds some women back, a broader "techno-logical aversion" may affect many more. Career counselors, for instance, report women clients asking, "Can you find me a field without computer printouts?"

Many women pursue educational and career paths that provide little technical training (a major in English instead of engineering, for instance) or little line experience (jobs in a business's moneymaking operations: production and sales). With women completing over thirty percent of all MBAs nationwide (in many leading schools, over forty percent), it's hard to say that they lack the necessary credentials for management. Still a disproportionate number wind up in specialist positions or staff tracks (in support units such as purchasing, advertising and personnel). This is due as much to prejudice as to preference. Believing that women dislike the "dirty work" that certain assignments entail (in manufacturing, for example), employers assign them elsewhere. Yet when opportunities open up, women have chosen these formerly off-limits jobs. In New York City recently, female municipal employees requested transfers from clean, safe desk jobs to the police and fire forces. Although some of the women suffered immediate pay cuts, all expected better advancement in their new jobs.

Carol Tropp Schreiber, Ph.D., manager of human resources, environmental forecasting and analysis for General Electric Corporation, devoted her doctoral dissertation to what happened when men entered so-called women's jobs and women entered stereotypically male jobs in a large utility company. She found that those who worked in transitional (cross-sex) roles were happier than if they had worked in traditional roles.

Roadblocks

Career progression may be even more important than career path. Removing yourself for even a short time from the pipeline—for marriage, motherhood, consulting, academia and sometimes, government service—may lessen your chances later on. No matter what term is applied to the phenomenon—topping out, dropping out, stopping out, opting out or copping out—corporations clearly resent it. The loss is particularly irritating to employers because of the training and replacement costs it represents.

Although the number of women making such moves may be small, the number of women affected may be quite large. "Topping out" raises, resurrects or reinforces questions about the career commitment and organizational loyalty of all women.

Women have yet to gain full acceptance in the office. Sometime old attitudes are submerged rather than changed. Male executives, for instance, may go to great lengths never to meet with a woman employee alone or behind closed doors. This practice might be termed "the gynecologist syndrome," since male physicians in that specialty seldom examine patients without a third party present.

When a company can't refuse to hire women outright, it still can cite difficulties of "client acceptance" to keep women out of certain key positions. Since "client acceptance" hasn't hindered women in such fields as industrial sales, I wonder if this is just a weak rationalization.

What Price, Success?

Women managers—once media darlings—are being discouraged from some quarters, so it is no wonder that they are beginning to question corporate careers. Some men still may view an achieving, accomplished mate as a social deficit or a personal affliction instead of a desirable asset. This concern centers largely on the question of who earns the greater salary. And anecdotal evidence suggests that women worry about this as much as men do. Some women have even declined promotions or placed ceilings on their sales commissions to keep their earnings down. One woman I worked with kept her $80,000 income a secret from husband until he had to sign form 1040.

Husbands can also feel conflicts and sabotage their wives'

work lives in subtle ways. Some might increase demands—for vacations or for home entertainment—at critical phases in their wives' careers. Others may belittle wives they fear might get too far. The outcome is often a psychologically battered wife.

One would hope, of course, that husbands could share in or, at least, support their wives' successes. Sadly, this doesn't always happen. When one advertising executive landed a major new client, she scheduled a celebration dinner with her husband at 8:00 p.m. Could it be a coincidence that he picked a fight at 7:00 p.m.?

The presumed price of success is a hot topic across the country. Press accounts of a Stanford University study of male and female MBAs warned women that the struggle to reach the executive suite may damage psyches. The finding that led to such headlines? Four times as many women as men had sought psychological counseling. But most articles on the study missed an important point. These findings may merely reflect the greater proportion of women that the medical and psychiatric professions refer for treatment.

Grace Baruch, Ph.D., and Rosalind Barnett, Ph.D., psychologists at the Wellesley Center, offer an excellent explanation of the attention now being paid to this subject. "Perhaps," they wrote in the *New York Times Magazine*, "there is a subliminal feeling that women who encroach on male territory are supposed to pay a price for it."

4 | IS BIGGER BETTER?

In this era of mergers and multinationals, it may seem surprising that most Americans don't work for large corporations. In fact, U.S. Census Bureau data indicates a trend toward working for smaller companies. Seventy-two percent of the work force was concentrated in concerns employing fewer than 500 people, in 1967. By 1979, this figure had increased to 78 percent.

Working for a small corporation may mean that the mention of your employer's name at a party will elicit blank stares instead of knowing nods. More important, an unknown employer may fail to impress the recruiter who scans your résumé. While salaries now are fairly competitive, small companies' benefit programs and resources cannot compare with those of large companies. Furthermore, if the company in question is family-owned, your chances of moving into the chief executive officer slot are next to nil, unless you marry the boss' son.

On the other hand, it's unlikely that you ever will feel you're just a number or a cog in the corporate machinery if you work for a company employing fewer than 500 people. It will be impossible, as well, to become invisible or overspecialized. You'll see results and probably get the glory you deserve. And it can be a great way to test your wings before you go out on your own.

It's A Small World

Bonnie Adamson clearly was taking a risk when she left 20th Century Fox to join the fledgling four-person Los Angeles office of Telepictures Corporation, a television program distributor. But because she knew those at the helm and thought highly of them, Adamson did not feel she was taking a big chance. "You hope against hope that a small company will make it," she says. Telepictures now employs 50 people and Adamson is director of operations in the international division. She has not regretted her decision.

Adamson acknowledges that she has to do more herself because Telepictures lacks separate sound and script departments, and other support services. In a small company, it is not unusual to send your secretary out to the store for supplies and to stay up until 2:00 a.m. preparing illustrations for a report. In a large company, explains Kieran Hackett, general partner in the RHE Group, a New York search and consulting firm, you just call the graphic-services department.

There is some danger of being a jack-of-all-trades and a master of none when you work for a small firm. Hackett has seen problems occur when one person is asked to manage too many functions. Small companies that lack a strong, vertical structure, notes Hackett, often must "get people with a lot of horizontal capabilities."

This can lead to a heavy workload. Arlynn Greenbaum worked for a number of large book publishers before joining the nine-person Eileen Prescott Company, Inc., a New York-based public-relations company, where she was vice-president. She recalls that "you get involved in many more aspects of business at the smaller companies." The long hours necessary in a small company can pay off. "Working in a smaller organization has given me the opportunity to be much more creative and independent. I was given increased responsibility at a point when you wouldn't get it in a larger concern," says Deborah R. Rocker, who became a vice-president of Intercapco, Inc., a Cleveland venture-capital company, at 27.

Greenbaum adds that larger companies may be a little staid for some tastes. "If I got someone on the 'Tonight' show at Prescott, I could scream. At McGraw-Hill, I would have had to put it in a memo." Rocker agrees: "In a larger organization, I always felt I had to watch what I did." Although she is more visible now that she works in a smaller company, Rocker feels there are fewer worries about not fitting into a mold. "Larger organizations tend to be more formal, and women feel it more. Some feel they must 'put their personality in the closet' before coming to work."

Greenbaum laments the lack of benefits at small companies. Although most firms now offer basic health and life insurance and a pension plan, only the largest ones offer innovative options, observes Robin Block, consulting actuary with the New York office of William M. Mercer, Incorporated, a benefits-consulting firm. Benefits such as vision-care coverage and group legal insurance, she notes, tend to "start at the largest firms and then trickle down." In fact, Greenbaum has recently accepted a position at a large publisher with more responsibility at higher compensation.

Where To Start?

Responsibilities may be broader at smaller companies, but formal training opportunities tend to be fewer. Lateral moves and overseas rotations usually are out of the question, and neither in-house seminars nor a budget for outside ones is likely. Instead of moving along a proven career path, "you must develop your own job as the company grows," says Anne-Marie Tardif, MBA, director of merchandise planning and control for L.L. Bean, Inc., a sporting-goods mail-order retailer in Freeport, Maine. If that route does not work out, there's often little you can do. You can't just transfer to another department because "there often isn't any other department," observes Joseph Giarraputo, publisher of *Venture: The Magazine for Entrepreneurs.*

Conventional wisdom suggests that it's best to start your career with a large company. Judith von Seldeneck, president of Diversified Search, Inc., a Philadelphia search firm, thinks "you're less marketable" coming out of a small company. Her banking clients, for instance, usually don't consider candidates from small banks, citing differences in the size of customer companies. If you come out of a major company, concedes J. Fredric Way, director of placement at Columbia University's Graduate School of Business in New York, you're more of a "known quantity."

While agreeing that it may be easier to move from a large firm to a small one than the other way around, Rosemary Kissel, a consultant at RW Consultants, a New York-based search firm, takes a more optimistic view. Kissel thinks small-company experience might be a plus in such areas as personnel and finance, where you'll get the generalist background that veterans of large companies lack. Kate Steichen, MBA, marketing manager for the traditional lines of games and toys at Parker Brothers of Beverly, Massachusetts, considers her earlier stint as director of a small art school invaluable. She feels she had greater responsibility sooner than she would have elsewhere and that she learned "to trust my instincts and make up the rules as I went."

It still is difficult, though less unusual, for new MBAs to go directly to small companies. Small companies are unlikely to have the resources to recruit on campus. However, more small companies are recruiting at business schools, and students are expressing interest in such opportunities, says Way.

Sizing Up A Company

If the small company you're considering is a subsidiary of a larger concern, ask yourself how prominently it figures in the profit picture and future plans of the parent, suggests Way. If it is a division or an outlying office, consider whether you can make your mark there or whether you'll be sentencing yourself to Siberia, he adds.

Examine the company as an investor or a venture capitalist would, advises Giarraputo. Look closely at top management, and "if you don't think it is awfully good, don't go with the company." Check out the growth prospects for the industry and evaluate the particular goods or services the company offers. Study the financing behind the firm. This may be difficult to do since small companies usually are not publicly held. Giarraputo suggests circumventing this obstacle by checking with competitors, and especially suppliers, to find out if the company pays its bills.

The trade press, local bankers and accountants, and the Chamber of Commerce all are good sources for names of small companies, according to Marilyn Moats Kennedy, author of *Salary Strategies: Everything You Need to Know to Get the Salary You Want* (Rawson, Wade). Kennedy suggests restricting your search to newer small companies. An older company that's still small, she explains, may be stagnant as well as unstable. Giarraputo concurs: "The trick is to join a small company that's not going to stay small."

5| OFFICE CLATTER

The rapid developments in video and audio teleconferencing, in print-based communication through keyboard terminals and the availability of portable minicomputers that can receive and transmit at a distance are making it technologically possible even now for enormous numbers of clerical, secretarial and white-collar tasks to be done from remote locations. And, since these are the very jobs that are estimated to make up 60 to 70 percent of the work force within the next 20 years, we could be facing an *enormous change in the way we work.*

Futurists extol this possibility as a boon for everyone, from the handicapped who find commuting cumbersome to mothers maintaining careers. But at least one environmental psychologist raises some questions about whether it would be so great to work at home. In *Workspace: Creating Environments in Organizations* (Praeger), Franklin D. Becker, an associate professor at Cornell University in Ithaca, New York, considers the role that the physical setting plays in behavior and speculates on the relative merits of *home-based versus office-based working.*

The interchange between people and setting—how they experience, modify and accommodate their environment—is the basis for the field of *environmental psychology.* The field borrows heavily from two more-established psychological sub-specialties: cognitive psychology (to understand perception) and social psychology (to understand interactions).

The importance of managers taking into consideration *the psychological aspect of planning a work environment* can be seen in a now-classic study on the relationship between working conditions and workers' productivity. In the Hawthorne studies—conducted in the late 1920s at the Western Electric Company's Hawthorne plant in Chicago, Illinois—lighting levels were varied and the corresponding gains or losses in productivity were recorded. The finding was that no matter how the lighting changed, productivity rose. The reason? The workers viewed all changes—more light, less light—as indicative of interest in them. *Their interpretation of the change mattered more than any particular change.*

"One of the reasons studying the work setting is neglected is because it's so obvious. You can touch it. You can paint it. It's just there," says Becker. Then, too, the psychological ramifications are seldom considered. *Work-place design typically is the province of the purchasing department,* which handles "things," rather than being the responsibility of the personnel department, which takes care of "people" needs. People forget that the things Purchasing buys affect the people Personnel manages.

Becker is concerned that visions of the so-called office of the future (such as those espoused by Alvin Toffler in *The Third Wave*) "tend to focus on equipment in a technological or abstract sense rather than on its implementation in real settings with real people."

Changes in how and where we work encompass more than just the physical space. According to Becker, it may involve changing our notions of workers and work.

Looking ahead, Becker foresees some unanticipated side effects when organizations try to solve their economic and energy problems by capitalizing on technological innovations that can *bring work into the home.* "For example," he says, "working at home via computer may reduce personal transportation costs, but it could require expensive changes in the size of design of the home to accommodate the new work patterns. It may reduce role conflicts with co-workers in the office, but it may create other role conflicts at home among family members."

Families, suggests Becker, already are snarled up in scheduling conflicts, trying to allocate limited resources to competing activities. "The introduction of work issues adds another layer of complexity and increases the potential for conflict."

Interdependence among co-workers also will change. Work in an office is based on the interdependence of jobs. Isolating workers means losing this interaction, which may lead to conflicts and need for *more* supervision. On the positive side, the absence of co-workers can make it necessary to pay greater attention to some centralized authority and force stricter attention to the individual worker's job performance.

To find out more about the conflicts, Becker and several of his students in the human-environment relations program of the Department of Design and Environmental analysis in Cornell's College of Human Ecology conducted a series of exploratory studies involving people who do part of their work at home:

• Student Lynn Bowlus studied *computer programmers.* Programmers tend to be "computer freaks," whose greatest difficulty, observes Becker, is in "doing something besides work." Co-workers who are not workaholics often feel at a competitive disadvantage. Based on Bowlus' findings, Becker says that the availability of home terminals may "exacerbate this kind of tension by implicitly suggesting that [additional] work should be done at home."

• Mary Anne McLaughlin studied *Tupperware dealers.* Conscious that their phones could ring at all hours and customers could drop in at any time, the dealers were concerned about being caught off guard and nervous about neatness. This concern carried over to their children, who were required to keep play areas neat and "clean enough for company" at all times. One of the dealers went so far as to buy a dishwasher, principally, she explained, "for hiding dirty dishes from unexpected visitors."

• Student Jana Reichle studied *stockbrokers,* who provided

an ideal sample since their work is the kind that should readily lend itself to being conducted at remote locations. Stockbrokers already receive most of their market information electronically and spend fully 50 percent of there office time on the telephone. But, far from cherishing the sounds of silence at home, some brokers missed the stimulation of the noise of the office. One went so far as to record the clattering and chattering sounds of the office so that she could play them back at home.

As technology allows organizations to adopt a home-based employment policy, employee personality traits and financial responsibilities to their work must be re-examined. Can a first-time employee be expected to learn good work habits at home? Will special programs be necessary to ease employees into varying career stages? And, even more crucial, will new standards of desirable worker characteristics emerge as others fade into obsolescence? Punctuality and group performance will not play as much of a role as independence and a tolerance for ambiguity in a job. Financially, new issues arise: For example, will an organization assume the responsibility for purchasing telephone lines, office equipment and supplies and additional storage space, or will the employee?

The trend toward home-based work is here to stay. The potential benefits are enormous, but Becker cautions us to study the inevitable side effects and to consider, now, who will benefit, how they benefit and at what cost to whom.

6 | CORPORATE PASSAGES

Traditionally, moving up has meant moving away from an area of specialization to enter management. Saleswomen become sales managers, teachers become department heads, reporters become editors. Management seems attractive because we glorify the power and prestige of managers. But, says one manager, it also means more "headaches and hassles," especially for women who are ill-equipped for the change.

Many women are surprised to find that dealing with people is much harder than dealing with projects. Women often enter chemistry, for instance, because they truly enjoy research—not because they want to file affirmative-action reports or testify at unemployment-compensation hearings, activities that may occupy scientists once they become laboratory managers. To make the transition to manager, then, first-line supervisors and other technical staff simultaneously must acquire new skills and relinquish old ones.

Trade-offs

"You have to be prepared to give up your strong technical skills," explains Jackie Barker, department manager at the Arden Hills, Minnesota, office of Control Data Corporation, a computer firm. Barker finds it valuable that she "speaks the same language" as her technically-trained subordinates and "knows enough to ask the right questions." But she also has had to accept that her own technical skills are becoming rusty, or even obsolete, and that she must give up the role of expert.

Managers also must learn to let go of previous responsibilities, and work with and through other people. Before becoming telecommunications project leader at Pfizer Inc., a pharmaceutical company in New York, Alexa McGill was used to doing everything herself. She knows the work of the staff members who report to her because she has held their jobs. But that knowledge initially has meant making "personal adjustments" as she has had to learn to delegate work.

Managers have to make other trade-offs, as well. Often they must give up the privilege of working at home or on a flexitime plan. Barker finds that technicians, specialists and professionals are better able to take advantage of such options than managers who must be available to others much of the time.

Transforming Yourself

Despite the trade-offs and difficult adjustments, the greater decision-making power, additional promotional paths and opportunity to earn more money can make the move to management worthwhile. To prepare for this step, first learn as much as you can about your own organization. Figure out which positions are the power seats. For instance, the general counsel of a corporation that does not rely heavily on outside law firms is in a much more powerful position than the general counsel of a corporation that turns to law firms frequently for advice.

Carefully consider your own aptitudes, attitudes and goals. Temperament may matter as much as, or even more, than talent. If you are a computer specialist who enjoys working autonomously, you might be miserable supervising a roomful of programmers. You might prefer to rise through the ranks as an in-house consultant, perhaps, or to join an independent management-consulting firm as a computer specialist.

Expect to develop a different style of working as a manager. Your ability to juggle simultaneous demands on your time will be tested as never before. And you will have to communicate differently, as well. "Technical personnel typically prepare memos and reports to convey information," says Mildred Myers, a lecturer in business administration at the Graduate School of Business at the University of Pittsburgh. Managers and executives put pen to paper for different purposes—to formalize a verbal request, perhaps, or to extend congratulations to create goodwill within the organization.

Managers may even have to learn new technical skills. Linda Schieber, a former librarian, is now the information manager at the United Nations Development Programme in New York, where she manages a group of five people who develop computerized data bases for UN documents. Schieber has not held any of the positions she supervises, but feels that she must know them in order to hire, train and monitor employees.

Remember that the transition to management will be taxing. Tackling a new job makes most people feel temporarily overwhelmed and exhausted. Not only are you mastering new tasks, but you are meeting new people, observes Meryl Reis Louis, Ph.D., assistant professor of organizational sciences at the Naval Postgraduate School in Monterey, California. In her recent article in the journal *Organizational Dynamics*, Louis explains that new managers must learn new jargon, create a new image and identity, foster new alliances and relationships, and untangle a new set of politics, in addition to doing their jobs.

Dual Ladders

Some specialists balk at becoming administrators, and employers, too, realize that good technicians do not always make good managers. As a result, alternative patterns of career progression have appeared. Some companies have instituted "dual ladders:" two parallel tracks that allow people to advance in status and salary either by remaining specialists or by becoming managers.

For instance, according to executive vice-president Larry

Hannah, the American Fletcher Bank in Indianapolis created the position of "senior commercial loan officer" to provide rewards and recognition for outstanding loan officers who prefer not to enter management.

Dual ladders seem to work better in theory than in practice. "The technical track will not lead you as high in the corporation as the managerial track," observes Laurie Michael Roth, Ph.D., a research associate at Columbia University's Graduate School of Business in New York. Compensation and noncash rewards (the visibility of making a presentation to the board of directors, for instance) go to those who follow the traditional managerial track. Roth finds that corporations do not look on employees who climb the technical ladder as people possessing a valuable set of specialized skills; rather, they view them as people lacking managerial ability.

In sum, employees climbing the technical ladder may feel as if they are second-class citizens. According to Meg Wheatley, assistant professor of management at Cambridge College in Massachusetts, "It seems that whenever there is a dual track, people know which track is the better one"; in fact, in all organizations, the "better" track continues to be the managerial route. And women who want to proceed smoothly on that track recognize that careful planning is the key.

7 | PRESTIGE PARADOX

It is no secret, as the latest U.S. Labor Department statistics confirm, that women still earn approximately 59 cents for every dollar men earn. Working women, in general, know this. But even when they acknowledge that sex discrimination may play a part in the salary disparity, they still do not think that they, personally, are discriminated against.

It is as though each woman considers herself the exception to the rule, explains Faye Crosby, Ph.D., who recently conducted a large-scale study of working women, non-working women and working men. Applying a group experience to your own situation may be a small step logically, she adds, but it is a huge one psychologically. If you consider yourself a victim of discrimination, you may be forced to regard your co-workers as the villains.

This is just one of the intriguing insights to emerge from Crosby's extensive interviews with 400 residents of one Boston suburb. Crosby, a 34-year-old assistant professor of psychology at Yale University, recently published her results in *Relative Deprivation and Working Women* (Oxford University Press, 1983).

Interestingly, notes Crosby, the pink-collar worker, who, objectively, may have the most grounds for complaint, is least likely to express discontentment over the way things are at work. Rather, it is women in more prestigious positions—executives and professionals—who tend to gripe more. Such women are likely to work with men and to compare themselves to their male colleagues. Having similar credentials, they may expect to do as well financially and grow disgruntled when they do not.

Working women also tend to talk more about how much they like their jobs, despite lower salaries. Accepting "psychic income" in lieu of financial rewards is not necessarily a good thing, according to Crosby. Women may continue to feel that they are entitled to only one or the other, but not both.

As more and more women accept the notion that they will be responsible for breadwinning through part or all of their lives, they will grow more concerned about inequities in opportunity, advancement and earnings. "It is in recent years, with job opportunities apparently expanding, that women have begun to express more vociferously than ever before their resentment about sex discrimination," says Crosby.

Another of Crosby's findings is that working women who are married and have children seem to enjoy their work more than those who are not wives and mothers. Much has been made of the multiple demands of filling so many roles simultaneously, but Crosby surmises that family life both enhances career satisfaction and puts job problems into perspective. "There may be nothing like relearning the multiplication tables at home with your kids to diminish the impact of trauma at work," she explains.

Crosby knows this from firsthand experience as well. She dedicated her book to her husband, Travis, a historian, and her sons Matthew, 8, and Timothy, 2. Her Yale office has the standard professorial bookshelves and blackboards but also has a container of Diaparene baby washcloths, evidence that her younger son is occasionally in residence. In that setting we spoke.

Marilyn Machlowitz: An appropriate place to begin, given the title of your book, is with a simple definition of relative deprivation.

Faye Crosby: Relative deprivation is a theory to explain feelings of resentment, deprivation and grievance. Common sense tells us that it's not just a matter of what we objectively have, it's also a matter of what we have relative to some standard—most probably other people. But if a sense of deprivation is relative to somebody else, then why aren't we always walking around feeling aggrieved? The issue of deservingness has to enter into it.

MM: Can you say a little more about that?

FC: The question seems to be: "Do we have what we think we deserve and what we want?" If we don't have something we think we deserve, then we'll feel upset and aggrieved. If we want something we don't think we deserve and we don't get it, we'll probably just feel depressed, sad or unhappy.

MM: What findings especially surprised you?

FC: The idea of job satisfaction being tied to a person's family status—single people are the least satisfied with their jobs. . . The people who love their jobs the most are the parents. [*Note:* Crosby's research sample included childless married people but not single parents. She will study them next.]

Several people have offered reasons for this. There's what's now called the "escape hypothesis": If you escape from home and go to the office, then you love it because you never appreciated how blissful and quiet it could be at the office until you had children at home.

I think that's true, but it works in another way. Multiple roles are very protective psychologically. If something goes wrong in one role, I can shut it out when I switch roles.

But if something good happens at work, I can tell my family about it at home and have much more pleasure than I would have if I went home and told the wall or the guppy.

MM: Were you surprised by anything else?

FC: The extent to which women refused to apply to their own life situation what they knew to be true in general. Everybody in my study had a sense of widespread sex discrimination [in salary], but women don't want to think of themselves as specific victims. There seems to be a real barrier. Now, logically, it would be to their benefit to know that they're discriminated against, but emotionally, psychologically, it would be at great cost. You don't want to think *you're* working with "meanies."

Now, women are not the only ones to be blind to their own victimization. The movie *The Garden of the Finzi-Continis* was a beautiful portrayal of European Jews denying the inevitable just prior to World War II. And we can all know statistically that one in four people is going to have cancer at some point, but surely it isn't going to be you or me. We have this protective shield of invulnerability around us.

MM: What about the future?

FC: First, I see the paradox of those having the most in terms of career being the least content. I see women being content with awful jobs and being content in the face of discrimination. But I think that as the number of women who are heads-of-household increases and as there are more professional families who could not live on one income, women will become ever more aware of injustices at work.

8 | LEAVING THE FAST LANE

For a long time it has been a given of the success ethic that an ambitious, bright executive should be constantly mobile.

Almost as soon as you start a new job, someone is sure to ask what you want to do next. Once you've been there awhile, you're bound to be asked when you're planning to leave. If you admit that you're satisfied and hope to stick around, you'll probably find yourself labeled "stale," "stalled" or "stuck."

Now there are signs that this trend is no longer universal. *Business Week* magazine reports that management women are dropping or "topping" out—reaching a certain level of career development and choosing to remain there. Judith Langer, president of Judith Langer Associates, Inc., a marketing-research firm in New York, agrees there's an increase in this "leveling off" trend among some professional women. Friends and clients admit that no, they don't want to become a chief executive officer. Concludes Martha Glenn Cox, Ph.D., assistant professor at Yale University's School of Organization and Management in New Haven, Connecticut: "More and more people at all levels in corporate America are deciding to stay put."

There are several reasons for these departures from the fast lane—social as well as economic. Many job changes require geographic moves. Even ambitious men and women are beginning to balk at the idea of relocation. The reasons range from the increase in dual-career couples to significant differences in mortgage rates from city to city. Furthermore, some people simply don't want to leave Danbury, Connecticut, for Davenport, Iowa, or vice versa. Others are giving their personal lives high priority. More responsibility, they say, "wouldn't be worth it," because they value their evenings and weekends too much.

The success ethic itself shows signs of change. Less emphasis on external measures and markers (such as salary and title) may militate against moving on or up, suggests Douglas T. Hall, Ph.D., professor of organizational behavior at Boston University's School of Management. He adds that promotions have lost some of the motivating power they once had, because of the prevalence of the two-income family: A $3,000 or $4,000 raise means much less to a family with a combined income of, say, $70,000 than to one with a single income of $35,000.

Changing Values

Professional pathways increasingly are open to challenge or, at least, questioning. Not every corporate engineer or psychologist wants to move up if doing so means moving away from one's discipline and into administration, report Ann Howard, Ph.D., and Douglas Bray, Ph.D., division manager and director, respectively, of basic human-resources research at the American Telephone and Telegraph Company in Morristown, New Jersey. Staying at one company does not necessarily mean that an employee is stagnating. Even when the company name on a woman's resume has not changed, her responsibilities, title and position may have. "Most social workers I know have moved fairly frequently, mostly out of frustration," notes a program administrator who has remained with one social-services organization since receiving her MSW (master of social work) in 1977. "But," she says, "I keep dealing with new problems and new issues. My position changes constantly, so in no way have I stagnated."

Sometimes, too, women "bypass that first step," explains Hall, and go straight to the sort of place they really want to work. They do this rather than starting out at a huge company famous for its training program and the mobility it allows you two years later. Susan Engel, M.B.A., senior associate at Booz,

Allen and Hamilton, a New York management-counsulting firm where she has worked since 1977, confirms that she and some of her colleagues joined the firm with the goal of becoming principals in about seven years. "By and large," she explains, "they don't regard it primarily as a place to put in time in order to 'leverage' oneself to a better job in industry."

Some women are content sticking with what they know and like, no matter what beckons from outside. "I've seen a lot of people who thought the grass was greener and they jumped and the grass wasn't greener," says Cande Olsen, an associate actuary who has worked for New York Life Insurance Company since graduating from college in 1972. She says, "I may have missed some opportunities, but I know that I like what I have."

Different Viewpoints

"Not moving is heretical for fast-track people," notes Jane Covey Brown, MBA, vice-president and director of planning for Goodmeasure, Inc., a management/consulting firm in Cambridge, Massachusetts. A woman at one of Brown's client companies was thinking of taking time off so that she could be with her newborn baby. The message she received was, "Don't do it." Similarly, at a major Chicago bank where Hall was conducting research, when a woman left to join a small, suburban bank, her former colleagues snickered, "That's not exactly life in the fast lane."

Although many professors and executives defend the decision to stay put, they also acknowledge that, for the most part, the fast track is still the accepted route to success. "A successful managerial career is based on much more than mobility, yet we focus on the mobility aspects," says Thomas P. Ference, Ph.D., professor of management at Columbia University in New York. "Mobility is not the only virtue," agrees Rosabeth Moss Kanter, Ph.D., professor of sociology at Yale University and chairperson of Goodmeasure, Inc.

If pressed, most people will grudgingly concede that, yes,

the good soldiers or solid citizens are the ones who keep most companies going. Yet few believe that employees willingly stay put. "The first week I got here, people started asking what I planned to do next," says Carin Rubenstein, Ph.D., associate editor of *Psychology Today* magazine, published in New York. Rubenstein resents such questions because of their underlying assumption that "anyone with a grain of talent is going to keep moving."

It is becoming widely recognized that organizations often hold people at certain levels. These people usually are termed "plateaued" or "put out to pasture." As far as top management is concerned, they are not going to be promoted above a certain level. In some instances, a position may be an end in itself. But individuals and organizations often base their decisions on other factors. For instance, if a woman is unsure of her goals, she may signal this unknowingly to superiors who then remove her name from the list of candidates for a promotion. Or, conversely, if an employer gives a woman a salary increase that is several percentage points short of what her peers receive, she may interpret this as a signal that her prospects for advancement are slim.

Dangers Of Downshifting

Should an employee plan to level off for a time—assuming the decision is hers to make—there are some risks to consider. Biases in terminology and training should not be overlooked. "One of the words that does us in is 'stuck,' " explains Natasha Josefowitz, Ph.D., professor of management at San Diego State University's College of Business in California. "Stuck means you're not upwardly mobile, the assumption being that upward mobility is what every woman should want," she says. MBA programs that rely on cases beginning "You are the chairman of a Fortune 500 corporation" are another problem, observes Ference. They reinforce the idea that everyone wants to be a chief executive officer at a top company.

Perhaps a bigger danger for women is that they will say they aren't interested in progressing, as a rationalization to "mask their self-doubts or their unwillingness to take risks," remarks Kanter. Cox confirms, "There is a danger that women are more likely to be satisfied with less than they should be."

Women may freeze themselves, Cox says, by believing that they are not smart enough or good enough for the next job (particularly if they are in awe of the incumbent), that they lack necessary credentials for it (and go back to school to overqualify themselves) or that they should possess *all* the skills a particular job ultimately will require before stepping into it. Cox counsels that a new job "should always be a stretch."

Some uncertainty, ambivalence and risk are inevitable when exchanging a known situation for a new one, and Cox is concerned that many women forget this. She worries, too, that women pass up opportunities to advance and then despair of ever getting ahead, without having allowed themselves to take the chance.

Women often worry needlessly that recruiters or prospective employers will look askance at a resume that reveals a lot of movement. Although some foreign firms still "look for longevity," says Bjorn F. Lindgren, president of BFL Associates, an executive-search firm in New York, many U.S. firms don't care if a candidate is an "opportunist" who has had a number of different jobs, so long as each was an upward move.

It may make sense to move on if your experience has been based on one organization's way of doing things or if the present job was also your first one. A woman who is a consultant in the New York office of Towers, Perrin, Forster & Crosby, a management-consulting firm where she has worked since receiving her MBA in 1975, plans to stay at TPF&C and hopes to become a partner fairly soon. Nonetheless, she does not dismiss the "image problem" of working where people remember the mistakes she made when she was only 22 years old.

It is important, too, to keep in mind the barriers women still face in advancing as far as men. Women, says Lindgren, "have to go upward as soon as possible. At this point, women have to move more."

9 | CREATIVE IMPERATIVE

When business is so concerned with productivity, nourishing creativity in the workplace may seem a luxury. Short-sighted managers may ask whether, in a no-frills economy, corporations can afford this "frill." But the real question is, can they afford to be without it?

"Creativity is the key to success and growth," says Eugene Raudsepp, president of Princeton (New Jersey) Creative Research, Inc. "It really is the name of the game these days." Raudsepp points out that today's rapid change—in technology, the economy, workers' value systems and the quality of work life—as well as the complexity of such problems as increasing foreign competition, decreasing productivity and the declining quality of products, call for creativity. This means greater flexibility in thinking and generating *many* solutions instead of just one.

That Nagging Twist

What is creativity, and how can it be nurtured? "To be creative," says Alice Rossi, Ph.D. (professor of sociology at the University of Massachusetts in Amherst), who has written and lectured on the topic, "means to break new ground, to synthesize opposites, to stand against the tides. When a creative idea or theory is so new as to cast doubt on long-cherished beliefs or styles, opposition to the new idea may be intense. To stand up to that opposition takes a fighting spirit and a tolerance for stress."

"Creativity," continues Rossi, "produces products that contribute something 'new' that is positively valued." It requires occasional total absorption in one's work, a tolerance for ambiguity and opposition, motivation, drive, energy and persistence, as well as native ability, appropriate training and relevant experience. And, she adds, it requires discontent. "Total happiness may yield smug satisfaction, acceptance of the world as a given, and so deprive the potentially creative person of that nagging twist in the heart or mind that motivates and spurs us to new thought and action."

Only 1 to 2 percent of the people in any given field are truly creative, by Rossi's criteria. Why are women poorly represented in the thin ranks of highly creative people? This is a result of lower female representation in the work force, not a lack of creativity. "There must be a large enough basic pool of women with the training and experience needed to enter a field," says Rossi, "if there is to be any realistic probability that women will make outstanding contributions." What, in Rossi's view, leads to creativity?

Talent, Training, Experience

Women may not have the background that is the basis of creative endeavors. Rossi observes that fields undergoing expansion of opportunities (for example, computer science, polymer science or chemical engineering) draw disproportionately from white males. Women and minorities enter fields that are contracting. "A decade ago," Rossi notes, "it was already clear that the market for legal talent or academic talent in the humanities or social sciences would be poor by the late 1970s and '80s. Young white males shifted to more lucrative and promising fields, while women have shown a rapid increase as a proportion of those seeking training in law, humanities and social sciences."

Life Priorities

"From all we know of the creative process from research

or from biographies of creative individuals," Rossi says, "it seems clear that work has been a major passion and a central, often exclusive, commitment of creative people." And recent studies of women's career histories, says Rossi, "show fewer and shorter breaks in careers even among those who bear one or two children."

Continuity And Persistence

The real issue is not simply withdrawal from and re-entry into the work force, but the possibility of periods of total absorption in one's work at summer institutes, advanced management programs, writers' colonies and the like. From personal experience—Rossi once spent a summer working during the night while the rest of the family slept, and she did not feel free to try a total retreat until her youngest child was 16—she feels that such periods of "total withdrawal from home" may be preferable to "working at home while trying to blot out domestic events and crises." Children, she thinks, still accept a distracted or absent father more readily than a similarly distant mother.

Motivation, Drive and Energy

Rossi notes that women used to feel free to express their ambition only as a "private confession," if at all. "More women today," she says, "feel free to express their ambition openly and to structure their lives in a way to pour most of their motivation and energy into their work." This will encourage greater creativity.

Experts differ in their assessment of the ease and usefulness of trying to become more creative. "The creative imperative," states Ethel Spector Person, M.D., a New York psychoanalyst, "is more easily prescribed than accomplished." Raudsepp, on the other hand, offers seminars on expanding one's creativity, to both corporate clients (including Hallmark, Dow-Jones, and

Arco) and to the public. Such programs, which typically last two days and cost $395 per person, emphasize overcoming the cognitive, emotional, perceptual and organizational blocks to creativity by problem-solving, exercises and games.

Considering the value of creativity, one would expect creative people to be among the most-valued members of any organization. Not necessarily. With the exception of such rarefied environments as advertising agencies and new-products divisions, creative people are viewed, says Raudsepp, "very ambivalently" and with "underlying anxiety." They're the ones, he says, who often are seen as likely to upset the apple cart, make waves, create change and question the status quo too much.

The implicit criticism in this is that creative people will not be predictable, will fail to fit in and will be hard to handle. The explicit message for creative people who want to function productively in the workplace is: (1) to document and detail even exotic schemes in the same tried-and-true, methodical way in which you would outline a staid business plan; (2) let others know what you are doing, to avoid surprises; (3) minimize eccentricity in dress and conduct; (4) frame questions constructively—challenges are appropriate, attacks are not; (5) leave prima donna behavior to the opera stars.

10 | REDEFINING LEADERSHIP

eadership—the process by which people influence others—
often is treated as though it were the same as management.
But not every manager must be a leader. This is particularly
true for those who are responsible for things—purchases, inventories, grounds or facilities—rather than people.

This is one of the changing notions of leadership to emerge
from a review of the last 30 years of research on leadership and
some relatively recent social changes: the movement of women
into management, a diminished regard for leaders, a seeming
decline of leadership qualities among managers, and the
importance of the often-forgotten follower.

The study of leadership—like so many other scholarly
pursuits—is subject to shifting fashions. It long had been
popular, for instance, to attribute different leadership styles to
gender and personality. Now, experts in the field are more likely
to ascribe such differences to status and situation.

No "Best" Style

"Male" leadership used to be deemed "better" than female
leadership because characteristics typical of the style—aggres-
sion, logic, autonomy, tough-mindedness—were considered
essential for success in top management. More recently, the
"female" model has been described as nurturant, consensual
(participatory), and far superior to the male style, explains
Martin Chemers, Ph.D., chairman of the psychology department
at the University of Utah in Salt Lake City. This reversal, he
adds, stems from "bias, not science. There is no scientific proof

that consensual leadership is universally effective. *No* style is always good."

A recent study by William Jurma, Ph.D., assistant professor of speech communication at Texas Christian University in Fort Worth, and Steven Alderton, Ph.D., assistant professor of communication at Wayne State University in Detroit, Michigan, "found that both male and female leaders used the same frequency of task-oriented communication, the same type of comments to regulate the flow of discussion and the same approach to giving and asking for information. Group members were equally satisfied with male and female leaders." Similarly, Chemers's own research has shown that "the idea of a grossly different distribution of leadership styles and behaviors across genders is wrong."

Additional research—mainly that conducted recently by Rosabeth Moss Kanter, Ph.D., professor of sociology at Yale University in New Haven, Connecticut—has revealed that what appeared to be sex differences were really power differences. Since gender and status were confounded (with women typically having less status), the notion of sex differences lingered, observes Paula Johnson, Ph.D., professor at the California School of Professional Psychology in Los Angeles.

But however baseless this bias, it seems to persist. "People expect women who are leaders to be different from male leaders," says Jacqueline Goodchilds, Ph.D., associate professor of psychology at the University of California at Los Angeles. Subordinates' expectations of and attitudes toward women in general affect both the group's actual performance and the followers' reactions to the leader's performance, according to a study conducted by Robert Rice, Ph.D., a former student of Chemers's who now teaches in the psychology department at the State University of New York at Buffalo. Rice's data indicate that people may expect a woman to be a less capable leader. When she proves to be otherwise, subordinates tend to be pleasantly surprised or angered that she failed to conform to stereotypes.

Task vs. People Orientation

To determine their particular leadership style, participants at business seminars and workshops may take standardized tests, quizzes, lists, true-or-false choices and others. Although Chemers has used such paper-and-pencil instruments and inventories, and acknowledges that they are popular with workshop participants, he says that other methods also are useful. He supports the work of his co-author, Fred Fiedler, Ph.D., professor of psychology at the University of Washington in Seattle, who has identified two types of leaders: those who are motivated toward accomplishing tasks and those who are motivated toward preserving relationships. The first type concentrates on getting the work done, without special consideration for subordinates' feelings in achieving a goal, the second type would prefer satisfaction on the part of everyone involved.

Fiedler, who has been studying leadership since 1951, contends that *both* the task-oriented and the relationship-oriented leadership style are effective. One style may work better, depending on the circumstances: how much support a leader has among her work group, how well the task is defined and how much legitimate authority the leader possesses.

Social Changes

The exercise of leadership is affected not only by its immediate environment but by its social and historical context, states Michael Maccoby, Ph.D., author of *The Leader*. Maccoby, who is a social psychologist and psychoanalyst in Washington, D.C., offered the Bell System as an example in a recent interview. One kind of sales leadership was necessary, he said, when the company enjoyed a near monopoly, but Bell requires another more innovative, more aggressive style of leadership now that it faces a more competitive marketplace.

Another cultural transformation affecting leadership, he

notes, is that leaders are less likely to receive automatic respect today. "Presidents, priests, professors and parents," he writes, "are no longer guaranteed deference." Recently, Maccoby explains, there have been widespread challenges to paternal authority in both the home and the workplace. This may be a result, in part, of more women heading households and entering business.

Leadership itself seems to be undergoing a transformation. Ann Howard, Ph.D., and Douglas Bray, Ph.D., division manager and director, respectively, of basic human resources research for the American Telegraph and Telephone Company in Morristown, New Jersey, have documented a decline in leadership. AT&T has conducted a series of studies of one group of managers since the 1950s and has been following a second group of managers since the '70s. Among the second, younger group, Howard has found a diminished desire to assume leadership roles or to get groups to accomplish goals, leading her to conclude that there is a "lapse of leadership motivation in the new generation of managers."

Currently, Fiedler is examining how leaders use their intelligence and their experience. So far, he has found only minimal correlations between leadership and experience. This may account for the existence of both plodding veterans and whiz kids. As he points out, "Joan of Arc was not very experienced."

Chemers is concerned with the frequently overlooked follower. His preliminary finding is that "opposite styles often lead to a much more effective managment unit" because then the manager and the subordinate pay attention to different aspects of a problem. Two task-oriented people, he says, are apt to "argue all the time" while two relationship-oriented ones might "spend all their time drinking coffee."

Better Leaders

Despite the idiom "born leader," all of the experts interviewed maintain that leadership skills can be sharpened. Here are some of their pointers:

• Fiedler suggests you try to modify your situation instead of yourself. You also should strive to get formal authority so you have the clout you need. Improve leader-member relations to secure informal group support as well.

• Don't only hire subordinates "in your own image." While working with such people may prove more comfortable initially, explains Chemers, it may prove less productive in the long run. When building teams or appointing task forces, he adds, make sure the membership includes both styles—those who are task-oriented and those more interested in preserving good relationships.

• Don't rescue others at your own expense, advises Pamela Butler, Ph.D., director of the Behavior Therapy Institute in Mill Valley, California. For example, she has found that women managers sometimes are reluctant to make even reasonable requests when they know that a subordinate has a personal problem.

• Try to offer leadership opportunities at all levels of an organization, Technical people showing interest in a leadership role long have been told to set their sights on jobs that offer more money and greater prestige, often at the expense of personal preferences. If a successful salesperson expresses an interest in a leadership role, make sure opportunities are available for responsibility in that area, and that the person doesn't have to move into supervision to advance. As Maccoby observes, "We've made it so that if you don't keep getting promoted, you're a failure."

• Remember, says Gordon Funk, director of organization consultation for Growth Associates in Newton, Kansas, that leadership is "only one component of management."

11 | GROOMING THE NEW ELITE

usiness schools are under pressure. Last spring, after years of escalating opportunities and growing starting salaries (more than $30,000 for some students), the 56,000 graduating MBAs marched straight into the recession: Fewer companies recruited fewer students for fewer jobs. In this tight market, placement offices also face the challenge of drumming up opportunities for a new breed of MBA—perhaps a woman who has worked for several years and wants to open her own business rather than the prototypical young man who wants to join a Fortune 500 company fresh out of school.

At the same time, business schools face criticism of the skills their newly-minted MBAs bring to the work place. The growing importance of international markets and competition, and shifts in the domestic economy and business environment, have led critics to demand that B-schools revamp their curricula. Business schools also are tapping into the "shadow" education market, estimated at $60 billion (everything from in-house corporate training courses to American Management Associations seminars). To do this, they are offering an array of executive-education programs that range from one day to one semester in length.

In recent interviews, the deans of six top business schools talked about how their schools are responding to these pressures. These deans form a disparate group. Some sound like the career academics they are. Others, reflecting a more corporate orientation, unselfconsciously describe their graduates as "our products." But for now, one characteristic unites them: their gender. In September 1983, when Elizabeth E. Bailey, vice chairperson of the Civil Aeronautics Board in Washington, D.C., took over as dean of the Graduate School of Industrial Administration at Carnegie-Mellon University in Pittsburgh, Pennsylvania, she became the first woman to head a major graduate business school.

Consensus and certainty are in short supply when deans discuss recent criticisms levied against MBAs. John C. Burton, dean of Columbia University's Graduate School of Business in New York, scoffs at charges that the B-schools are turning out shortsighted, highly-specialized technicians. "That's an assertion repeated frequently enough to be thought a fact," he says. "I don't believe the evidence supports the assertion." Columbia, like most other schools, offers extensive training in the "soft" fields such as policy and strategy as well as in such "hard" areas as operations research, he explains.

Donald Carroll, dean of the University of Pennsylvania's Wharton School in Philadelphia, also disagrees with the charge that today's MBAs are "cold" technicians, citing Reginald Jones, recently retired chairman of the board at General Electric Company, and Leonard Lauder, chief executive at Estée Lauder, Inc., prominent Wharton alumni, as counterexamples. Carroll points out that Wharton students study such soft areas as strategic and long-range planning. In fact, he believes that Wharton should place additional emphasis on planning and studying real situations, through applied-research centers and supervised consulting opportunities.

Burton also dismisses the accusation that today's MBAs are ill-prepared to meet the challenge of increased international competition. "It doesn't seem to me that there's a big difference in dealing with competition wherever it comes from," he contends. But other universities disagree. They are increasing their international offerings. "Wharton's newly-created Center for International Management Studies and our international business program are reviewing current international offerings and examining how international components can be introduced into basic functional courses such as labor, finance and accounting," says Carroll.

Critics also charge that women's needs in business school, and in business itself, differ from those of men and that B-schools do not recognize this difference. Carroll is hard-nosed about sex-segregated study. "Wharton's own female MBA population has soared from just 2 percent of the total a decade ago to fully one-third today—and without special attention to the 'women's issues' of business. Our approach has been that women and men need the same training and face the same hurdles in both business school and in business."

Only one business school in the U.S.—the Graduate School of Management at Simmons College in Boston, Massachusetts— is intended specifically for women. Simmons considers non-academic achievements in admissions—for example, a housewife who has raised children and been an active community volunteer might be a likely candidate. Penny Martin, director of admissions at Simmons, reports that Simmons gives women a sense of confidence and helps them to establish their credibility immediately. Simmons offers classes on how to deal with the problems faced by women in business. Surveys of Simmons' alumnae show that they delight in their new-found "number-crunching" ability when they graduate. Martin finds that graduates value their behavioral skills even more after four or five years because their technical competence has become a "given" on the job.

Covering New Ground

In response to market demands for updates in business disciplines, business schools are moving into entirely new areas. Carroll says that Wharton has "greatly expanded the number of joint-degree programs we offer, in recognition of the growing importance of interdisciplinary approaches to increasingly complex problems. Now students can combine their MBAs with advanced degrees in law, medicine, international affairs, engineering, urban policy and nursing."

Yale University's School of Organization and Management in New Haven, Connecticut, plans to offer new courses on legal issues and dealing with lawyers, according to Dean Burton Malkiel. Yale's program integrates corporate and governmental concerns, and Malkiel finds that alumni appreciate this "public-private mix." Yale also has added an extensive program in organizational behavior. Malkiel observes that "human-resource problems are going to be among the most important ones faced by business people in the years ahead." Graduates of the school benefit from the "sensitivity and skills they have developed with respect to 'people problems,'" through these courses, he explains.

The list of new areas now covered in the business-school curriculum keeps growing. Yale has added courses in small-business management, and Harvard recently added a professorship in entrepreneurship. But Columbia's Burton questions these offerings. "Entrepreneurship is difficult to teach someone," he asserts. "If someone has the bent, then his or her ability will be enhanced by having an MBA."

At New York University's Graduate School of Business Administration in New York, courses on ethics have been in the spotlight lately. Dean William May wonders whether the subject matter may be too specific to U.S. culture and standards. "I don't know if American business ethics *should* prevail," he says. But he concedes that these courses have proven popular with students.

As much as deans differ on the kinds of courses to add to the curriculum, they agree that MBAs need better communication skills. "If the Wharton School could offer just one course to future managers," says Carroll, "I'd want it to be our program in communications. One of the most important skills a manager can have is the ability to communicate clearly and succinctly.

Part of the problem in improving the communications skills of managers, though, is their general inability to recognize the importance of competent communications. They know when they don't understand a problem in finance, accounting or some other functional area, but frequently can't recognize when they've written a completely abstruse memorandum."

Laws of Supply and Demand

Several deans believe that the decline in recruiting has been overstated. "There is a group of elite schools whose students always have been in great demand and, I think, they always will be," explains Richard Rosett, dean of the University of Chicago's Graduate School of Business. "Even during an engineering glut," he continues, "the MIT graduate still gets a job."

"For schools below the top tier," cautions Wharton's Carroll, "the situation is quite different. Recruiters are cutting back on visits to them, and there probably will be some shake-out in the number of such schools offering the degree."

The large-company emphasis in organized on-campus recruiting is likely to continue. Small companies cannot compete with the salaries large companies offer, nor is it economical for small companies to establish relationships with large B-schools when their recruiting needs may mean hiring only one person every three years, explains Burton. Such "institutional barriers," he concedes, "are hard to lower."

One Final Question

Debate about curriculum and recruitment aside, should working women enroll in graduate business programs? Burton believes that a brief educational program, an evening MBA program or even a full-fledged, full-time MBA program may not guarantee a magic career boost, but he agrees with other deans that a business school background is helpful.

Rosett observes that women who enroll in evening MBA programs with the expectation that their employers will promote them when they graduate are all too often disappointed. "Not every firm needs, values or wants the education you get at a top-flight business school," he continues. Women MBAs may be able to get better employment elsewhere with the extra credentials, though, just as men do, he says.

Short programs have both advantages and disadvantages. Carroll points out that a short program can provide adequate exposure to a different discipline or emerging technical field. Many people could benefit from a passing acquaintance with accounting, but most don't need to become CPAs, he explains. Brief programs also can increase a person's credibility on the job. On the other hand, "a six-week course is not an MBA degree, so if women are competing for jobs against MBA candidates, their credentials still won't measure up," he warns.

The deans agree that the doom and gloom should not dissuade well-qualified people from enrolling in top MBA programs. May believes that the new frontiers afforded by the Third World and by the new technology offer continuing opportunities for MBAs.

12 | WORKAHOLISM

When Riva Poor, a Cambridge, Massachusetts, counselor and consultant, wrote *4 Days, 40 Hours* (a book that advocated shorter work weeks), she was working almost 20 hours a day, seven days a week. Poor said, "I wrote a book that helped people have lots of leisure, but I wasn't having any."

There have always been women workaholics. If housework had been recognized as work, generations of compulsive cleaners would have been considered workaholics. But today, women's workaholism becomes readily apparent as more and more women enter and advance in business and the professions.

The word "workaholism" is found in magazine quizzes more frequently than in research literature. The few scholarly statements on workaholism and workaholics have tended to condemn the phenomenon and criticize the people to whom the term applies. While psychiatrists may call them anxious, guilt-ridden or self-destructive, workaholics themselves (and many management experts) hold more sanguine views. Anne Hyde, president of Management Woman, Inc. (a search firm specializing in women executives) and a workaholic herself, attributed workaholism to ambition and asked, "What's wrong with that?"

Indeed, meeting energetic, enthusiastic workaholics made me speculate that workaholism is not as bad as has been believed. My efforts to define workaholism and to distinguish workaholics from other hard workers proved difficult. While workaholics do work hard, not all hard workers are workaholics. Moonlighters, for example, may work 16 hours a day to make ends meet, but most of them will stop working that hard when their financial circumstances permit. Accountants, too, seem to work non-stop, but many slow down after the April 15th tax deadline. Workaholics, on the other hand, *always* devote more time and thought to their work than their situation demands. Even in the absence of deadlines to meet, mortgages to pay, promotions to earn, or bosses to please, workaholics still work hard. What sets them apart is their attitude toward work, not the number of hours they work.

Workaholism manifests itself in the following ways:

For workaholics, work is integral to, and often indistinguishable from the rest of their lives. While some workaholics are reluctant to admit that's what they are (because of the pejorative stereotype still associated with the term), few resent the dominant role of work in their lives or even feel overworked. Sally MacKinnon, a group brand manager for R.J. Reynolds Tobacco Co., in Winston-Salem, North Carolina, said, "I don't feel that I have to put in the hours I do (7:30 a.m. to 6:30 p.m.). I've never thought of the time I work as a sacrifice because there's nothing I'd rather be doing."

The personal and professional lives of workaholics are frequently intertwined. "Some of my best friends are people I've met over a conference table . . . and some of my clients are people I've met at parties," explained Laurel Cutler, senior vice-president for marketing planning at Leber Katz Partners, a New York advertising agency. "The joy of my job," continued Cutler, "is that no two days are ever alike."

Workaholics thrive on variety. Elizabeth Whelan, Sc.D., for example, is a research associate at the Harvard School of Public Health. In addition to conducting research on epidemiology and public health, Whelan consults and writes on a broad range of topics for both popular and professional audiences, directs The American Council on Science and Health, and moderates a syndicated radio program, *Healthline.*

Workaholics find inactivity intolerable. "I get very depressed and moody if I have nothing to do," admitted the president of a New England real estate firm. Cutler concurred: "I'm miserable when I don't have enough pressure." Much of the pressure on a workaholic stems from her own willingness to assume additional activities. "I'm complimented when people want me to write something or give a speech," Cutler said. Similarly, the real estate woman conceded she is over-committed. "I accept too many responsibilities. I tend to overdo it. I have trouble saying 'No.' " The inability to say "no" is typical. Workaholics often feel inadequate or insecure. The real estate woman admitted, "Even being successful in business hasn't eradicated my insecurity." No matter how undeserved such suspicions are, they may propel workaholics to try to please others and to earn their approval by attempting to fulfill every request.

On the other hand, overinvolvement can be a conscious career strategy. Many women feel excluded from "the old boy network," locker room conversations and other informal channels of communication. They seek ways to compensate for such exclusion. Monica Bauer, program manager in marketing operations for Xerox in Rochester, New York, explained, "I really did have to put in more time than my male associates just to get the information." Lizette Weiss, director of public affairs for the Metropolitan Transportation Commission in Berkeley, California, finds professional organizations particularly valuable for this purpose. By becoming active in the American Society for Public Administration, Weiss has met many of the senior people in her field and has developed a nationwide network of professional contacts.

Unable to be idle, workaholics seem to hate having free time. Workaholics structure their time carefully and stick to their schedules. Cluttered calendars of days committed—and overcommitted—are filled weeks in advance. They refuse to waste even a minute. Lizette Weiss always carries something to read, "so if I have to wait, I don't have to twiddle my thumbs." Workaholics are extremely organized and efficient. Whelan begins each day "with a detailed list of everything to be accomplished." (She freely admits her principal time-waster may be looking for lost lists.)

Indeed, workaholics employ so many time-saving techniques simultaneously that saving time sometimes becomes a goal in itself. Riva Poor exercises by cycling to appointments. Keeping commuting time to a minimum is a conscious strategy. Florence Haseltine, M.D., an assistant professor of obstetrics and gynecology at Yale University, likes living in New Haven in part, "because my home, office, hospital and lab are all within a five minutes' drive of each other." Haseltine also stretches her time by delegating or eliminating whatever extraneous duties she can. Regarding housework, Haseltine said, "I have a very simple solution: I don't do any." Having earned part of her own college and medical school expenses as a maid, she has no qualms about paying someone else to clean her house.

For workaholics, vacations are hard to take. At least one psychiatrist prescribes vacations for his workaholic patients—many of whom have accumulated months of unused vacation time. Restful vacations make most workaholics restless. They survive by combining work and play while away. "Even on vacation, I have my typewriter with me," explained Whelan, author of nine books and numerous articles. Haseltine relaxes by attending medical meetings in exotic locales. It is a milestone when workaholics can take—and actually enjoy—a vacation. A few years ago, Poor tried her first three-day weekend and, to her surprise, liked it.

The pattern of workaholism appears in childhood. Parents play a part in its origin and onset. Monica Bauer of Xerox remembered her parents' expectation that she "exceed and excel." Whelan recalled that her parents "always rewarded achievement and encouraged me to go to Yale and Harvard," where she earned her graduate degrees. "Ironically, when I got all the degrees they'd expected and finally got married, they wanted me to quit work and start having babies."

Concerns about bearing and caring for children distinguish women workaholics—and working women, in general—from their male counterparts. Whelan, whose books include *A Baby? ...Maybe: A Guide to Making the Most Fateful Decision of Your Life* had her first child last July and has hired a full-time baby nurse. Still, she said, "I simply cannot understand how anyone could have a second child. I am exhausted!" Although her husband, a corporate attorney whose 12-hour workdays match hers, tries to do his part, Whelan contended, "He can't help out, as most husbands can't, no matter what is said about 'joint responsibility.' "

It is these interpersonal relationships—with husband, children and friends—that suffer the strain of women's workaholism. As Golda Meir told a reporter for *The New York Times:* "Somebody said I was married to my jobs...my children suffered at various times, but when they got older, they understood. As for my husband, he was a wonderful human being. Bad luck that he married me."

Workaholics are often accused of working to the exclusion of other human needs. In *The Journal of School Health*, Drs. William Masters and Virginia Johnson report that their work-addicted patients either "exalt work to the highest priority in their lives and relegate sex to the lowest, or they approach their sex in fundamentally the same (goal-directed) fashion as they do their work."

When workaholism results in recognition and financial rewards—as it often does—additional problems can occur. The real estate woman referred to marital problems as "the dues women have to pay." Now separated from her husband, she recalled that her involvement in work was "fine with him, at first, when I wasn't earning much money." Shirley Polykoff, a New York advertising executive, never allowed her salary to exceed her husband's. When he died, her employer, Foote, Cone

& Belding, immediately doubled her salary and, shortly thereafter, doubled it again. She explained, "It wasn't good strategy for a woman to be too successful."

Workaholism is probably permanent. Even compulsory retirement could not stop Polykoff. Five years ago, after retiring from Foote, Cone & Belding (where she had created such advertising classics as "Does She...Or Doesn't She?"), Polykoff started her own agency. Now president of Shirley Polykoff Advertising in New York, she still has no plans to slow down. "I'm doing more now than I've ever done. I don't know how you retire if you're still healthy and exuberant about living. They'll have to carry me out in a box."

Even if their "affliction" is ongoing, not all workaholics realize their "plight" is supposed to be a problem. Many would agree with Winston Churchill who once said, "Those whose work and pleasures are one are fortune's favorite children."

PART THREE

Traps That Can Trip You Up

13 | THE GREAT IMPOSTERS

W hy do so many accomplished women attribute their success to luck or good timing?
• Laura, a summa cum laude Princeton graduate, insisted that her admission to Harvard Business School was the result of a computer mistake.

• Lisa, a Philadelphia teacher, agonized before taking a test to become a department head and then received the highest score in the city.

• Paula, an award-winning actuary, thought that her recent promotion stemmed from her sunny smile and perky personality.

Laura, Lisa and Paula—like many other capable, accomplished women—doubt or discount their own abilities and achievements. Despite firm evidence that they are successful—from high SAT scores to good sales figures—these women feel that they do *not* do well and that they will fail in the future. Moreover, they believe that they have fooled anyone who thinks otherwise.

The price these women pay for their doubts is excessive anxiety, limited enjoyment of any accomplishments, and—in extreme cases—curtailed careers. Women who experience this "impostor phenomenon" have fled from law school on the first day or turned down challenging job offers.

In less extreme cases, those who feel they are impostors may seize every chance to reveal something unnecessary and negative about themselves. When someone says, "I was fired from my first job," years after the fact, or "I almost flunked my computer courses" when appointed to a task force on information systems, she's convinced that her successes were strictly flukes, and she wants to warn you that fiascos will surely follow.

Another device that many self-styled impostors adopt is procrastination. "When you leave things to the last minute, the result doesn't reflect your potential, but rather your skill at brinkmanship," explains Jane Burka, Ph.D., a psychologist at the Counseling Center at the University of California at Berkeley. Procrastination prevents "having your best efforts come to light and be evaluated. It is painful and yet protective. If the results are good, you may feel fraudulent. If the results accurately reflect your lack of time or effort, you have a protective built-in excuse."

When so-called impostors do slip up, they feel a surprising sense of relief. Pam, a lawyer, failed the bar exam the first time she took it. She felt glad, She says, that " 'they' had finally caught up with me."

How It Starts

Men experience the impostor phenomenon, but the pattern is far more pronounced among women. Studies such as those by Kay Deaux, Ph.D., professor of psychology at Purdue University in West Lafayette, Indiana, show that women are more likely to seek external or temporary explanations for success. A musician may attribute her success to a terrific teacher rather than to her own talent. A judge may say that she was "in the right place at the right time" rather than that she was "a damn good lawyer."

As a result, a woman may more easily accept external or situational explanations that *others* offer for her success. When a woman advances, then overhears unfounded remarks such as, "She slept her way to the top" or "She was just an affirmative-action hire," she may wonder about her actual ability. Similarly, if a woman has been complimented for her appearance far more than for her competence, she may not realize she possesses both attributes, notes Jean Wellington, Ph.D., associate professor of psychology at Tufts University, in Medford, Massachusetts.

With all the mixed messages society sends about success—especially women's success—almost any woman is apt to feel at least a little ambivalent about it. Denying or sabotaging your accomplishments and achievements means you can avoid dealing with the "problem" of success. This may be why "the brighter the woman, the more she seems to suffer" from the impostor phenomenon, observes Inge Broverman, Ph.D., director of the division of psychology at the University of Massachusetts Medical Center in Worcester, Massachusetts.

Parents contribute to the onset of the impostor phenomenon, too. Some women remember being told that they were the "beauty" of the family while a sister was the "brain." Or a woman may have heard that she had the academic skills, but her brother had the social graces. Women who grew up with these myths may not even be aware of the conflict they feel between their desires to dispel these myths and their need to prove them true, explain Pauline Rose Clance, Ph.D., associate professor of psychology at Georgia State University in Atlanta, and Suzanne Imes, Ph.D., an Atlanta psychotherapist. Whenever a woman's actions contradict her family's myths, she may look for more acceptable explanations: "It was a fluke," or "It must not have been that difficult."

Clance and Imes also have encountered women who grew up hearing that they were superior in every way and who felt that everything always came easily to them. Their parents may have bragged that their daughters walked when they were 1 year old, talked at 2, read at 3, and played the piano at 4. When such a woman learns that certain endeavors require effort, she may begin to doubt her "superior" abilities.

What To Do

Once the impostor phenomenon starts, it sticks. "We have been amazed at the self-perpetuating nature of the impostor phenomenon," write Clance and Imes. Even repeated successes, they add, do not seem to break the belief. What can work, they say, is concerted effort. First, accept your accomplishments and attributes, even if doing so entails changing a long-standing view of yourself. Just because Mom or your math teacher didn't think you were a whiz, that doesn't mean you can't count. Don't carry around a dated self-image that no longer fits. Just as a formerly fat woman often heads automatically to the size 16's and has to steer herself to the size 10's, you may have to remind yourself of who you are now.

Second, explain your successes in terms of your actions and abilities. In other words, "own" your accomplishments, don't throw them away by attributing all your achievements to timing or luck.

Third, keep track of compliments you receive and observe how you dismiss, discount or distort them. Compliment other women on their work and listen to them do the same thing. To keep the compliments coming, try to avoid the tendency to mention all of your troubles and none of your triumphs.

Fourth, talk about the impostor phenomenon with friends. You probably will learn that you're not alone, notes Imes, who, with Clance, has conducted several workshops on the subject. If you attend a women's group or belong to a network, suggest using this article as a springboard for discussion.

Fifth, don't hold yourself to impossibly high standards. Often, observes Clance, an adequate performance is all that's necessary. Remember this when you persevere or procrastinate over routine tasks. Perfectionism, in such instances, is counterproductive.

Sixth, imagine yourself telling everyone you think you've fooled exactly how you did so. Imes suggests starting with the most recent situation and going as far back as you must. Imagine yourself telling an admirer from an audience, "You thought my speech was good? You probably can't hear very well," and realize how absurd and arrogant you sound. Think how much better "Thank you" would be.

14 | COPING WITH AMBIVALENCE

Male executives don't usually have to be reassured that gender and achievement can harmonize, and if they do, there's plenty of research to show that "lucky at work means lucky in love." But for women, who have only recently exchanged the fear of success for anxieties about life at the top, there's less literature to give reassurance against pervasive and sometimes self-defeating ambivalence. There's also the fear that a successful professional life will stand in the way of a meaningful personal life. Are you short-changing your husband and children when you take a high-level, high-pressure job? Will you betray your gentler instincts by locking horns with a male co-worker? Does the emotional distance you maintain as an effective supervisor cripple your ability for intimacy outside the office?

Dealing with such ambivalence day in and day out, women often suffer from stress, anxiety and depression. What's more, says Tufts University psychologist Jean Wellington, "This ambivalence undoubtedly exacerbates women's secondary positions in the work world."

The good news is that serious researchers, such as Barrie Greiff and Preston Munter of Harvard, authors of *Tradeoffs*, say that "femininity and success are absolutely compatible." The danger, though, is that unresolved ambivalence can weaken a woman's sense of herself. This muddled mental state may spark questions at work about her commitment to her career. If it's conveyed to bosses and colleagues, ambivalence can undermine a manager's confidence in a woman as an employee, or detract from how she's seen as a member of a team.

Good Start, Bad Results: Paradoxically, an early brush with success can increase ambivalence in adulthood. Robin Post, a clinical psychologist and assistant professor in the psychiatry department at the University of Colorado School of Medicine, says that dependency conflicts rank high among the problems facing the female graduate students she counsels.

The conflicted women had little emotional support from family and friends as girls. They were looking for parental approval, according to Post, by achieving at high levels. The more they succeeded, the less support they received, precisely because they seemed to be successful and self-assured. "These high-achieving women find themselves caught in a struggle between their wish to be self-sufficient help-givers and their own unmet needs for affection and nurturance," says Post.

"They feel lonely and inadequate," she continues. "Most said they had never experienced a satisfying relationship with a man. All were single." Ironically most of Post's patients were studying to be physicians, people who take care of others but remain professionally detached.

Diane Hill, a Denver psychotherapist who teaches at the University of Colorado School of Medicine, traces the origin of ambivalence to adolescence. Explains Hill: "Before girls reach puberty, achievement is a pretty reliable way to get praise, love and affection. Afterward, the pressure to continue achieving at their present rate of excellence collides with pressures to be more 'feminine,' more social and more affiliative."

Awareness of ambivalence is the first step toward accepting what may include unacceptable feelings—"I don't like my colleagues" or "I'm smarter than my boss." Wellington stresses the need for a woman to understand her own wants, priorities and the messages she is sending. She helps her clients see that achievement and attachment to others are *not* mutually exclusive.

When women are asked to imagine circumstances that would force them to choose between home and work, they realize that they don't have to sacrifice one for the other unless the imaginary situation became a reality. Says Wellington, "Many women feel compelled to make choices even when a choice is not forced." Ambiguity is tolerable so long as it's not accompanied by ambivalence.

The doubts that plague career women about their identities fall into four categories that psychologist Jean Wellington has recognized. She relates each one to a pattern of probable consequences:

1. *Sexual identity.* The woman values success but equates it with masculinity. This raises the specter of losing one's feminine sexual identity as the price for attaining career goals.

2. *Superwoman syndrome.* There's pressure to perform both domestically and occupationally. Role confusion may result: Am I a banker who is a mother or a mother who is a banker? Added to this ambivalence is rage at role overload.

3. *Liberation credo.* It's necessary first to assess which of the divergent ideals of the female role, traditional or classic, she is most comfortable with. Then she feels compelled to choose between them.

4. *Flirting/flaunting strategy.* Using femininity to get ahead in business may work in the short term, but in the long run it feeds self-doubts about competence.

15 | THE SURVIVOR SYNDROME

In this era of layoffs, cutbacks, RIFs (reductions in force) and furloughs, there are a growing number of invisible victims. People who lose their jobs often receive outplacement services, unemployment compensation and sympathy, as they should. But those who retain their jobs receive little or no attention or assistance.

Yet survivors suffer, too. The term "survivor syndrome" first was applied to the guilt and grief of people spared by Hiroshima, the Holocaust or a hurricane. Today's recession should not be compared to those disasters, but it does take a toll. While no one would rather be fired than spared, few survivors react as positively as one might expect.

"Everyday life at work is drastically different once a layoff occurs," says Paula Rayman, Ph.D., assistant professor of sociology at Brandeis University in Waltham, Massachusetts. Employees miss familiar faces on the coffee line and no longer assume that job security is a certainty. The mere threat of job loss has many of the same emotional effects as actual job loss, concludes Leonard Greenhalgh, Ph.D., an organizational psychologist and associate professor at the Amos Tuck School of Business Administration at Dartmouth College in Hanover, New Hampshire.

Survivors tend to withdraw from customary social and civic activities and often feel vulnerable, betrayed and isolated. They also feel that they have lost, permanently, any ability to predict or control the course of their careers. Team spirit goes by the board because survivors tend to look out for themselves. Office morale and productivity plummet. Management's assurances that a particular layoff will be the last frequently fall on deaf ears. Survivors anticipate additional layoffs and wonder whether they will be spared a second time.

Layoffs can affect a survivor's ability to do her job and progress in her career. Reducing personnel by five percent may trim some unnecessary fat. On the other hand, it can put a crimp in an entire operation. Remaining employees may have to work overtime to maintain their previous output, or they may have to curtail efforts in certain areas or ax some services totally. A cutback of ten percent can cripple or even kill a program, explains Donald A. Seckler, Ph.D., a clinical psychologist in Cambridge, Massachusetts, who consults for several organizations including the Boston Police Department and the *Boston Globe* newspaper.

Issues of importance to women—sexual harassment, affirmative action, occupational safety and health—may get pushed to the side. Some women, who selected companies or fields that they thought would offer a safe harbor or a fast-track career, are angry that opportunities for advancement have slowed or shrunk. As Sandra Lyness, Ph.D., a clinical psychologist and associate professor at Wayne State University in Detroit, Michigan, says, "Just when a lot of women were beginning to go up the corporate ladders, many are finding that there is nowhere to go."

Survivors' Stories

Survivors react to their uncertain situations in various ways. Some reduce risk taking: They won't challenge superiors, suggest innovations or otherwise rock the boat. They grow anxious about keeping the jobs they do have and may wind up feeling locked in, says Rayman.

Judy Linscott, a reporter for the *Daily News* in New York, felt "pulled in two directions" when layoffs hit her newspaper. "I wanted to listen to colleagues who had received pink slips,"

"Linscott says, "but it was difficult to get work done." With fewer people and the same number of pages to produce, there was more work for those remaining. Linscott thinks that the editors acknowledged the increased workload more than the emotional turmoil the survivors faced. She thinks the process took its toll on the editors, too.

Rebecca Rochell, who is now director of development for the Phoenix House Foundation, Inc., a residential treatment and prevention program for drug rehabilitation based in New York, once had the kind of job crisis everyone fears. After her children grew up, Rochell became a fund raiser for one of New York's leading cultural institutions. She had only been on the job for a short time when her department was reorganized. Six months later, she was the only remaining member of the original staff.

"Initially," Rochell recalls, "I was relieved, because I didn't want to be fired from my first job." Later, when she began to wonder why she had been spared, she concluded that her inexperience meant she "was not a threat to anybody." This shook her self-confidence.

The concept of a survivor syndrome had never occurred to Rochell until she experienced it herself. "I never imagined that being a survivor could be hard," she says. She felt guilty that her good fortune (the new management promoted her) came at the expense of others. "The work atmosphere was intolerable. Any ability to function as a team was gone. People think of themselves when their own jobs are on the line," she concludes.

How To Prosper

Some women adopt aggressive strategies in the wake of a layoff. Once her Fortune 500 company started retrenching, one woman manager decided that "this was not the time to hide my light under a bushel basket." She began showing superiors more of what she could do, even at the risk of violating corporate protocol and seeming brash. Comparing herself to a slave on the auction block, she has started lobbying for an internal transfer to a more profitable section of the corporation. She regards these tactics as preferable to alleviating her anxiety by joining in unproductive group gripe-and-gossip sessions.

You may find that your chances for advancement actually improve after a layoff or reorganization. A consulting firm recently demoted some of its senior consultants who lacked the credentials of newer employees. So while one 28-year-old woman felt sympathetic to those whose careers had been derailed, she knew that the move was a good one for her.

Even if a layoff leaves you with greater autonomy (your boss has been let go) or responsibility (two peers have been axed), try not to spread yourself too thin. If you wind up feeling overwhelmed, you'll lessen your own effectiveness. Ask your supervisor which directions to pursue so that you don't wind up charging at full speed into the wrong areas.

Should you find yourself with new responsibilities or seek such a reassignment, be careful to avoid areas where your weaknesses outnumber your strengths. In general, try to steer clear of "developmental" situations—assignments where you are expected to know little and to learn a lot—in favor of those where your talents will shine. (Of course, new recruits may have little choice.) Marginal performers are likely to lose out even during good times, but especially during hard times. Seek as much information as you can when word of an impending layoff leaks out, says Abby Watel, MSW, a psychotherapist at the Elk Grove Schaumburg Townships Mental Health Center in Elk Grove, Illinois. Facing unpleasant facts ("There may be further layoffs") is better than imprisoning yourself with the worst scenarios your imagination will provide ("We'll all be fired with two days' notice and no severance pay"). Relying only on rumors, says Watel, is often what fosters panic. When you learn what's in store, you can examine your options and act on your own behalf.

Watel also advises her clients to change careers when future prospects appear grim. One woman worked in the travel industry and, after surviving a layoff, concluded that her whole field was in trouble. She decided to break into another industry.

Even women who remain in their fields and don't seek transfers should arm themselves with new skills to provide for future contingencies, claims Lyness, a Detroit psychologist. It might be a good idea to learn administrative skills, master computer usage or polish up your mediation skills.

Do not resign from professional societies or civic groups. Contacts can help "recession-proof" you, and they should pay off no matter which way the economy turns.

Managers who survive layoffs have to worry not only about their own situations but about their subordinates as well. The executive director of a nonprofit organization explains how tough it is to preside over a mass termination. She and her aides, she says, underwent "incredible personal anguish" and were "virtually unable" to make the decision to dismiss employees. They conducted an exhaustive—and exhausting—search for options, held long meetings rehashing alternatives, went without sleep, made the final "agonizing" choice and now—more than a year later—still try to justify their actions to themselves.

When you have to handle survivors, advises James J. Gallagher, Ph.D., chairman of J.J. Gallagher Associates, an outplacement firm in New York, decide on standards for determining which employees are to be retained. Plan how you will present the information to those let go, those kept on and (if your firm is prominent in your area) the press. There is no perfect way to inform people. If you use group meetings, some participants will regard them as impersonal. If you tell people individually, the gossip will get to most people before you do. A good rule of thumb is to tell the terminated people before the others and to make sure the first word comes from you personally, not from a newspaper or memo.

Follow up immediately, suggests Gallagher, with written information on the terms of termination: severance pay, the sequence in which people will be rehired (if applicable). Then, make every effort to reassure remaining employees, paying particularly close attention to those who worked side by side with people who now are gone.

Paying attention to the survivors of a layoff is new. No systematic research has been conducted yet on the phenomenon and, in telephone interviews across the country, I had to explain my conception of the problem again and again. But the issue of survivorship—which affects all of us indirectly—will not go away. Preparing for the grief and guilt may minimize its impact.

16 | THE SOCIAL WORKER SYNDROME

One of the first lessons of the women's movement was that women needed to overcome their tendencies toward passivity and dependency in order to make it in management. The model executive, after all, was a tough, independent, outspoken man. "Assertiveness training" became a household term, and countless women bought books or attended seminars that promised to teach them to be "assertive, not aggressive." Today, neither the problem of passivity nor its alleged cure of assertiveness receives much attention from management theorists, feminists or women managers themselves. But some women still act in stereotypically feminine ways, keeping the Girl Scout vow of service to others even when it's inappropriate.

No one would deny that sensitivity and unselfishness are valuable qualities. But woman who stress these over all other qualities may lose sight of managerial goals and risk jeopardizing their careers. "Many women are trained to put other people's needs ahead of their own," observes Maria Villas-Boas Bowen, Ph.D., a clinical psychologist in private practice in Solanas Beach, California. Women managers define others' needs and desires as legitimate but consider their own unimportant. I call women's tendency toward self-denial the social worker syndrome (at the risk of offending an entire profession).

Company Saints

The causes of the syndrome are easy to diagnose. One, of course, is the way women are socialized. As psychotherapists Luise Eichenbaum and Susie Orbach have pointed out in their recently published books, *Understanding Women: A Feminist Psychoanalytic Approach* (Basic Books) and *What Do Women Want: Exploding the Myth of Dependency* (Coward-McCann), women are reared to become nurturers upon whom others can depend. And Robin Dee Post, Ph.D., a clinical psychologist and associate professor of psychiatry at the University of Colorado School of Medicine in Denver, notes that high-achieving women are more comfortable helping others and deny their own needs or hesitate to ask for aid.

Another reason that women managers tend to be company saints is their desire to be appreciated, praised and liked. "Women are known as conflict avoiders, peacemakers and approval seekers," says Natasha Josefowitz, Ph.D., a professor of management at San Diego State University and the author of *Paths to Power* (Addison-Wesley). Many women find it easier to accede to a co-worker's excessive demands than to risk confrontation and alienation by reasoning or arguing with the person.

A third cause of women's corporate self-effacement is a desire to counteract or compensate for "unfeminine" levels of achievement. Women in senior positions who feel guilty about their success may try to seem "womanly" by acting obliging and modest.

That co-workers often expect women managers to be resident social workers only exacerbates the syndrome. Josefowitz's research shows that subordinates look on their women bosses as surrogate nannies or mothers. Subordinates expect women managers to keep their office doors open, accept phone calls at home, put up with interruptions and grant extensions on projects. And while nannies and mothers have some authority, children usually can count on their indulgence. So, too, co-workers count on the good nature of their staff "mothers." "Social worker tendencies can subvert legitimate authority relationships," says an officer at a major New York financial-services institution. To counteract her staff's assumption that she always will accommodate them, she finds it useful to demonstrate her technical proficiency, to act tough and not to make allowances for poor or late work.

Professional advancement and financial rewards may be curtailed if a woman falls prey to the social worker syndrome. An ambitious attorney, for example, who fears that it isn't "right" for her to aspire to become a highly-paid partner in a prestigious firm, may choose the less lucrative realm of the Legal Aid Society. "The view that women are good or ought to be . . . 'good' usually translates as 'too good'—too good for politicking and therefore governing, too good to make deals and therefore to enter business," writes sociologist Cynthia Fuchs Epstein, Ph.D., in her 1981 book, *Women in Law* (Basic Books). "As a result," Epstein continues, "women have been encouraged to perform 'good works,' which, typically, are low in prestige and poor in career potential."

And while "nice" women managers may enjoy friendly work relationships, their careers often go nowhere. An assistant professor, for example, recently was denied an expected promotion because, in a setting where research is the name of the game, she had failed to publish enough scholarly papers. Instead, she spent her time outside class with students—revising their résumés, listening to their problems. While her students sing her praises, they do not make promotion decisions.

The personal price of being an executive social worker also can be high. Women who read subordinates' first drafts instead of insisting upon final versions, or otherwise allow themselves to become the victims of upward delegation, end up working at night and on weekends. Then, too, striving to consider everyone's feelings at all times makes it hard to arrive at decisions. If decision making becomes too painful, women may postpone or avoid it, hardly the style of an effective manager.

Women who kick the social worker habit pay a price for their nonconformity, though. Kathryn M. Bartol, Ph.D., and David A. Butterfield, Ph.D., report in the *Journal of Applied*

Psychology that different standards are used to evaluate male and female managers with identical leadership styles. Bartol and Butterfield asked 312 male and female business students to evaluate the performance of male and female managers in several case studies. One study told of a new manager who quickly reorganized a department. When the new manager had a male name, the students gave him high ratings. When the manager had a female name, she got lower ratings, possibly because she seemed too "pushy."

Other studies have confirmed that women managers who do not behave in a "feminine" fashion are penalized. According to Carl Camden, Ph.D., assistant professor of communications at Cleveland State University in Ohio, who studied offices managed by women, "Women who conform to stereotypically male management styles are negatively perceived." A department functions smoothly and subordinates perform well and advance, Camden found, only when women managers conform to subordinates' expectations by showing concern for others and promoting office harmony.

Androgynous Future?

It sounds like a no-win situation: Women who act like social workers aren't respected, and women who act like stereotypical macho managers are condemned. The only possible solution is to abandon the whole notion that there are male and female styles. In *The Androgynous Manager* (AMACOM), management consultant Alice G. Sargent proposes doing just that. She predicts that future management styles will combine masculine and feminine qualities. Eventually management will become wholly androgynous, with no distinction between male and female styles, and the very concept of androgyny will fade away. Sargent cites as one sign of the coming revolution the new management theories and textbooks holding that managers must be just as good at dealing with people as they are at linear programming or computer analysis.

Even if Sargent's revolution never occurs, increasing numbers of theorists and executives now recognize that sexist managerial stereotypes, like all stereotypes, simply are wrong, especially for women who have succeeded in becoming leaders. Veronica Nieva, Ph.D., and Barbara Gutek, Ph.D., authors of *Women and Work: A Psychological Perspective* (Praeger), have concluded, after much research, that "women in leadership positions function similarly to men in the same circumstances." As more women reach high executive positions, their example will discourage other women from adopting "social worker" behavior.

Nieva and Gutek's work, then, seems to buttress Sargent's prediction that male and female management styles are converging. The day when both sexes will be free to strike their own balances between their personalities and the demands and expectations of others may be closer than we think.

17 | WORK, MARRIAGE AND DIVORCE

When Lori B. Andrews, a Chicago lawyer, announced her plans to get married, her colleagues at an international conference shook their heads and said, "Well, I guess we won't be seeing you anymore." Andrews was surprised that they assumed her marriage meant she no longer would travel on business.

• When a 40-year-old accountant married for the first time, her partners behaved as though they had been betrayed. The accountant feels that her partners thought of the firm as her surrogate spouse, since she had spent 20 years there. Having a real husband, she surmises, made her something of a bigamist in her partners' eyes.

• When a manager in Kansas City, Missouri, separated from her husband, her co-workers took turns walking into her office and interrupting her train of thought by demanding "How *are* you?" Although they undoubtedly thought they were being sympathetic and supportive, their efforts had the opposite effect. "They made me more depressed," the manager says.

Most working women regard their marital status as irrelevant to their careers and are surprised when a marriage or a divorce affects their work lives. As the cases of these three women show, though, the repercussions can be serious, or at least uncomfortable. Because sociologists and psychologists have done little research on this issue, women still have to rely on the experiences of other women (often the best guide in any case). So I talked to a number of recently married or divorced women to find out how corporate America reacts to changes in marital status.

Traditional Beliefs

I found discouraging evidence that a traditional mind-set (holding that a woman's commitments to her career and her marriage are mutually exclusive) predominates in many industries and regions. A woman who announces her marriage plans still can expect to be asked whether she will continue to work. In *Paths to Power* (Addison-Wesley), Natasha Josefowitz, Ph.D., a professor of management at the College of Business at San Diego State University, discusses the stereotypes that women managers still must fight. For example, if a man has a picture of his family on his desk at work, co-workers will assume he's a "solid, responsible family man." If a woman puts a family portrait on her desk, co-workers assume that she is announcing that her family comes before her career. In other words, employers view marriage as a stabilizing force for men but not for women.

In fact, my research reveals that when women marry, their work performance either is unaffected or zooms upward. Several women report that having a husband requires far less time than their previous pattern of dating several men at a time. And preliminary research done by Faye Crosby, Ph.D., an associate professor of psychology at Yale University, indicates that although the relation between divorce and work performance varies from person to person, divorced men's work may suffer more than that of divorced women. Some women put so much energy into trying to save a doomed marriage that the trauma of separation and divorce drains them completely and their work takes a nose-dive. After the divorce, though, they flourish and their work improves. Crosby suspects that, in these cases, divorce frees the women from a difficult situation, allowing them to concentrate on their careers.

The encouraging news is that women themselves typically have far less trouble handling a change in personal circumstances than their co-workers and employers do. In fact, a woman's greatest problem often is to manage others' reactions, not her own. And some women are lucky enough to work in progressive companies where managing co-workers' reactions isn't hard. Nehama Jacobs, an advertising executive in New York, maintains that no one in her agency batted an eye when she announced that she was getting married or later when she got divorced.

Managing Change

The consensus among the women I interviewed was that the key to handling a change in marital status is to take control of the situation and convey competence and confidence in your ability to manage the shift in your personal life. You also need to transcend stereotypes. Otherwise, you run the risk that your marriage or divorce will have professional penalties—lost opportunities for travel or training, for instance—regardless of its personal rewards.

Disclose decisions appropriately. If a reorganization or promotion is in the works, it might be better to wait to announce marriage or divorce plans. If, for example, you have been nominated for a challenging new job and your boss learns that your personal life is in flux, he or she may choose someone else. Your boss may think it too risky to assign key tasks to someone who's undergoing a period of adjustment.

Delay telling co-workers of plans until you have answers to questions that will come up. It is better to have firm answers to queries about a new name or address than to shrug one's shoulders, says Ellen Freudenheim, an assistant vice-president at Chemical Bank in New York, who got married earlier this year. Unclear answers about your married name, for example, may lead to awkward business introductions later, as co-workers struggle to recall your preference.

Decide who should be told. Obviously, office protocol dictates that you tell your boss first. And the benefits department will have to know in order to change aspects of your insurance, pension and health coverage. But you may not want to tell anyone else. A good rule of thumb is that if the news will reach someone through the grapevine, it is more polite to tell that person yourself.

Keep a low profile. One manager did not even try to keep her stormy separation a secret. Now that her promotion appears to have been delayed for a year, she feels that her candor was a mistake. A lawyer I know used her secretary as a part-time wedding consultant and made frequent phone calls to her mother. In retrospect, she, too, feels that her behavior tarnished her professional image.

Conversely, Lori Andrews, the Chicago lawyer, did not tell anyone at work that she was getting married. She simply returned from her vacation wearing a wedding band. When people noticed and commented, she confirmed that she had gotten married. Andrews kept her marriage private because she believes that a woman's personal life is often used against her at work.

The best approach lies between giving daily bulletins and maintaining total secrecy. Freudenheim offers sound advice: Talk about a wedding (or divorce) no more—and no less—than about any other personal details.

Pulling Your Weight

Don't try people's patience. Don't use work associates as amateur psychiatrists. Save long and personal discussions for friends and relatives. And don't hesitate to seek professional help to ease the transition. At work, it's important to maintain your customary appearance and competence. If you stop pulling your weight while continuing to draw a paycheck, co-workers may grumble. Most of them, and most bosses, will make allowances for short periods. The duration of that period depends on how long you have worked there and how well you have performed in the past. Unfortunately, their patience may not last as long as you wish. So if you begin to feel fretful or frantic, take a few days off.

Expect changes in your relationships with male colleagues. When you are a newlywed, your old gang might not include you in their Friday evening "happy hour." If you want to continue to go along, you'll have to make the overture. When you are newly separated, a male lunch buddy may pull back for awhile or, instead, may come on to you. Again, it's up to you to send the signals.

Don't overreact. Some separated women treat every flirtatious remark as though it were an episode of sexual harassment. It is likely that you will be much more alert to sexual innuendo whether there is more coming your way or not, suggests Robert S. Weiss, Ph.D., professor of sociology at the University of Massachusetts in Boston, and the foremost researcher on separation and divorce.

Be prepared for some surprising or paradoxical reactions, too. Some women report an upsurge in sexual advances as soon as they start wearing a wedding ring, perhaps because men believe that they now can make overtures safely, with the assurance that they will be rebuffed because the women already are "taken," and not because the women think these flirtatious men are undesirable.

Don't feel that you have to fit a stereotype. You may have to go out of your way to show people that you are willing to break with tradition. Even if you marry a man who is wealthy, be sure to indicate that your income still is important. Andrews offers a kidding rejoinder to those who suggest that she can afford to earn less now that she is married. She jokes that her husband was hoping that her earnings would permit him to retire.

Be sure to broadcast your willingness to travel on business or attend training sessions out of town to contradict assumptions that you must stay at home, advises Andrews.

Most women I talked to find that it is stereotypes, and not the change in marital status, that unsettle them more. It is "other people's image of what a wife should be" that poses problems for Andrews, not her husband's or her own images.

Those conference colleagues of Andrews' who didn't expect her to leave Chicago after she got married probably were surprised to learn that she made a solo business trip almost immediately after her marriage. She and her husband returned separately from their honeymoon in South America so that Andrews could attend to business in New York.

18 | OCCUPATIONAL OVERFLOW

When Laurada Byers, an executive recruiter in Philadelphia, moved into her new house, she was delighted to learn that her next-door neighbor was a banker. Because Byers' firm, Diversified Search, Inc., conducts searches for several banks, she thought, "Maybe he can become a client."

Many managers find that what they do for a living affects the rest of their lives. We all are familiar with the indirect effects of our work: We may remain tired on tense after a pressure-filled day or elated if a project has gone well. But many of us are not conscious of our work's direct effects when we transfer managerial skills and styles to our after-hours life.

Managers disagree about what constitutes undesirable carry-over. Most would find fault with the network television correspondent who pontificates during pillow talk as well as on the screen. Quite a few would object to the lawyer who argues in her own house as though she were still in the courthouse.

Besides such obviously destructive transfers, there are no absolutes. Even the loquacious TV correspondent may be irritated when she is asked to expound over her breakfast tray during a 6:30 a.m. flight. Yet the contentious attorney may find her negotiating skills advantageous when seeking estimates for an addition to her house. What is at issue, then, is not whether we are "on" after hours, but whether being "on" contaminates or enhances our life.

Setting Limits

Occupational overflow stems from a variety of sources. "A compulsive need to excel in an occupational role" can make that role encroach on people's other life roles, explained the late Talcott Parsons, the noted sociologist at Harvard University, in his book *The Social System* (Free Press). Accordingly, people who are anxious about their performance or their competence may try to prove themselves whenever and wherever possible.

Then, too, the overflow that seems to be linked to a person's job really may spring from the person herself. Rather than being an occupational hazard, the overflow may be a matter of personal style. Even before Byers became a headhunter, she enjoyed putting people in touch with one another.

When overflow does result from the job itself, it may relate to properties of the position—for instance, high status—that have little to do with the content of the job. The nervous newcomer may feel compelled to perform all the time to compensate for her inexperience. Paradoxically, a well-established woman also may feel that she must adopt a professional manner at all times.

Finally, overflow can be caused by the expectations of others. A doctor is presented with symptoms and asked for diagnoses wherever she goes, and she always is presumed to be interested in hearing about everyone's operations. Then, too, a woman's personality, her job and outside expectations may combine to create the occupational overlap. So the college president who is new to the position and intent on doing well may strive to behave in a manner that suits her new role—and she will find that others expect her to fit this mold as well.

Managers must learn to expect occupational overflow at certain stages of their careers. The enthusiasm of the newly converted—for instance, the manager whose department recently has gone on-line and who sees opportunities for computerization wherever she turns—is inevitable and understandable. So, too, the member of a corporate task force on sexual harassment may find herself especially alert to conversational nuances that she overlooked before.

After these initial stages, managers need to relax. The person whose work requires extensive formal education—such as a doctor—or whose work receives great deference—such as a corporate treasurer or a federal judge—needs to "take off her cap and gown" when she returns home, says Mortimer R. Feinberg, Ph.D., chairman of the board of BFS Psychological Associates, a management-consulting firm in New York. For example, if you are prominent in your industry, you may discover that the social gatherings you attend grow stiff because everyone is afraid to relax around you. You might want to crack a joke or introduce a topic for conversation that is entirely unrelated to your profession, so that everyone feels equally entitled to venture opinions.

You may want to build in buffer zones as you shed one role for another. Rosalind Barnett, Ph.D., a clinical psychologist in private practice in Weston, Massachusetts, and the co-author of *Lifeprints* (McGraw-Hill), requires time to herself after listening to patients all day. She tries to block off some time when she does not have to respond to the needs of family, friends or anyone else.

Other professionals try to set boundaries between work and leisure activities. "I try never to spend my free time in a store," explains Pam Fields, a buyer for Bloomingdale's New York store. "After being in a store for that many hours, the last thing I want to do is shop." Similarly, two distinguished professors pull on rumpled clothes on weekends and watch birds or search for wild mushrooms.

A Small Price To Pay?

All too often, though, "there isn't *enough* spill-over between a woman's professional and personal life," says Jay Rohrlich, M.D., a psychiatrist in private practice in New York and the author of *Work and Love: The Crucial Balance* (Harmony

Books). Rohrlich finds that patients who fell insecure about their analytic and capable demeanor at work may act fearful, dependent and compliant at home.

Techniques and practices that prove useful on the job may be employed at home as well. Deborah Rocker, vice-president of Intercapco, Inc., a venture-capital firm in Cleveland, manages investments in small and medium-size businesses. She believes that moving their resources around all day helps her to handle her own admittedly more modest finances. And executives who go to seminars to learn how to manage stress, master time or deal with anger at work have been known to use the same techniques at home. Occupational overflow offers benefits for your work life, too. Jane Whitney, who anchored her own weekday television program in Philadelphia until recently, got comments from viewers wherever she went, and she sometimes wound up with good ideas for future shows.

Don't apologize if you enjoy being "on duty" much of the time. One physician's associate, who is part of the paramedical team at a major New York hospital, is bombarded with health-related queries from her friends. She enjoys answering the questions she can, and referring the rest to doctors.

Although it can be annoying to be interrogated outside your office about your work, the tendency to quiz working women means that women are being taken seriously. This trend is quite encouraging in a country where reporters asked the first female astronaut if she would wear a bra while in flight instead of what kind of scientific equipment she would use. The occasional annoyance is a small price to pay for society's overdue, though still self-conscious, recognition that women hold significant positions, possess considerable expertise and wield increasing power.

19 | YOUNGER BOSSES

Although age long has been associated with authority, this is less and less the case. "Society has become accustomed to the 28-year-old mayor and the 30-year-old college president," writes Bernice Neugarten, Ph.D., professor of education and sociology at Northwestern University in Evanston, Illinois. In the business world, we see more and more young people managing those older than themselves. Demographic changes, new corporate policies, technological advances and various social shifts have all contributed to this trend.

Although employers and employees alike may be able to see the reasons behind the trend, both groups sometimes feel uncomfortable in their new roles. Those who swiftly outpace their elders for a place on the "fast track" may feel a bit strange the first time they supervise people who look like their parents. Others may remember preparing to meet a new boss and finding themselves face-to-face with a fresh-faced "kid" instead of the gray-haired eminence they expected.

When a boss is not only younger but female, the tensions often are even worse. When young men are in positions of authority, they violate only one set of norms—those relating to age. Young women, on the other hand, violate two—those relating to age and to sex.

The demand for new training (particularly in high-technology fields) coupled with the insistence on additional credentials (for example, MBA degrees) tops the list of factors leading to the rise of the younger boss. Social shifts—such as women re-entering the work force after their child-rearing years, the vast numbers of "baby boomers" (those born during the 15 years after World War II) moving into middle management, the small but increasing tendency to start a second career in middle age—also play their parts. Corporate policy is evolving to de-emphasize seniority (in nonunion situations) in favor of ability, and this too contributes to the trend.

Baby boom vs. Depression kids. For the person facing a younger boss for the first time, three separate sets of feelings occur in sequence. First, the psychological: possible bruised pride. Second, the political: the sense of being "blocked" by someone younger, so that opportunities narrow for you. Third, the practical: goals and values may conflict.

A younger boss, then, needs to be sensitive to the older employee's feelings and attitudes. "One of the most important things for a younger person to be aware of is the value system of a person ten, twenty or thirty years older," points out Art Strohmer, director of human-resources planning and development for Merck & Co., Inc., a pharmaceutical company. So-called Depression kids (roughly, those now over 45) learned to expect self-denial while baby boomers (roughly, those under 35) feel entitled to self-fulfillment.

Older subordinates often assume that a new, younger boss "won't know her stuff" and will have to be trained by them. The person reporting to a boss younger than herself needs to adopt a "wait-and-see attitude," says Strohmer, reserving evaluation and avoiding a chip on the shoulder.

Ellen Unger, now a 37-year-old associate claims analyst for a large life insurance firm, successfully dealt with this situation. When she first returned to work after raising her son, she dreaded working for someone younger than herself. Then she realized that such people usually had many more years of work experience than she did. Now, says Unger, "If they know the job, I don't mind if they're younger."

Outsiders brought in over other people's heads frequently face more resistance from their subordinates than those who've risen through the ranks. When Sheryl Foxman, 32, first joined the Cleveland metals company of which she was vice-president until recently, she found supervising older subordinates quite difficult. "The men, especially, recoiled at my telling them what to do," she recalls. One quit, in fact.

"Work groups still are not used to a woman in authority, whatever her age," explains Lynn Kahn, Ph.D., a San Francisco organizational consultant. When the work group has not reported to a woman before and the woman has not managed before, the problems mount up, notes Carol Beauvais, Ph.D., a psychologist in Florence, Massachusetts.

When one of Beauvais' clients—a 30-year-old woman— was brought in over the heads of several older men, she encountered outright insubordination. The man who thought the job should have been his refused routinely to follow orders. When she eventually fired him, he came to work the next day anyway. He left only after the woman's boss (a man) told him to.

Inexperience obviously can affect a young manager's style. Playing power games when you're not quite sure how much power you have, or pretending to know it all when you don't, are tendencies that backfire, observes Sharon Kirkman Donegan, executive vice-president of Boyle/Kirkman Associates, Inc., a Boston-based management-consulting firm.

Even graduates of prestigious business schools may know more about management-in-theory than management-in-practice, notes John Zenger, D.B.A., president of Zenger-Miller, a Menlo Park, California, training firm. He considers it a mistake to move young people into managerial roles without giving them specific training in the nuts and bolts of supervision.

How to cope. It is important for a young manager to realize that adverse reactions may not be directed at her personally. They are more apt to be the ritualistic response of groups to any new authority figure, explains Kahn. If you recall how your elementary school class misbehaved whenever a substitute teacher was there, you can understand better that the antics and "acting out" have little do with you.

It is a mistake, though, to try to prevent such reactions by reducing your own authority. One young cosmetics company manager became chummy with an employee close to her age. When the manager had to give her friend negative performance reviews or withhold information about sensitive organizational issues, she saw the friendship and the work relations fizzle.

Nor is it smart to retreat to the role of "daughter." Doing so may make it seem difficult or dangerous to discipline "daddy." Conversely, you may find yourself becoming as aggressive and argumentative with "mommy" as actual adolescent daughters often are, observes Carol Nadelson, M.D., professor of psychiatry at Tufts–New England Medical Center.

To make sure that any adverse responses to you as a leader are short-lived, start out on the right foot. Show firmly that subordinates are expected to submit the reports you require and attend the meetings you call. Let them know, advises Kahn, that you will not ignore any failures to cooperate. Be tactful about the age discrepancy and don't draw attention to it. Stay out of the where-were-you-when discussions, lest you remind your subordinates that they were in college but you were only in elementary school when President Kennedy was assassinated.

Convey a sense of competence and confidence, counsels Marcia Kleiman, co-director of Options for Women, a Philadelphia career advisory and consulting firm. Try not to communicate the uncertainties you undoubtedly feel. Save these feelings for family, friends, or even a formal support group.

Do not hesitate, however, to select older subordinates. Unlike the situation when you're brought in over their heads, "when you hire them," confirms Foxman, "it's no problem."

Expect, too, to see changes in the world of work as the trend toward younger bosses continues, says Strohmer. Having been exposed to rapid advances throughout their lives, today's younger managers will be less tolerant of bureaucratic "red tape" and more apt to "want to make things happen." And they undoubtedly will.

20 | CORPORATE HUSBANDS

A merican women expect to find in their husbands a perfection that English women only hope to find in their butlers," wrote W. Somerset Maugham. How are today's executive, entrepreneurial and professional women doing in their search? No one knows. Existing surveys of working women are based on such small samples that their findings may not represent the rest of the population. And these small-scale surveys show that fewer than half of such women are married, a statistic that restricts research possibilities further. Studies that rely on large, national samples are out-of-date; they reflect the biases of a time when married working women were far less common than they are today.

Because two-career couples have become a permanent social institution, the need for information about them is pressing. Although much work remains to be done, we can draw some preliminary generalizations and guidelines about corporate marriages.

Many kinds of men marry corporate women and, obviously, "what may be ideal for one woman may be completely wrong for another," states Clifford J. Sager, M.D., a psychiatrist and noted marital therapist in New York. Men married to managerial women do tend to fall into four categories, though, says Maryanne Vandervelde, Ph.D., president of Pioneer Management, Inc., a management-consulting firm in New York. Some husbands achieve as much (or more) than their wives, while others do not. And whether or not they themselves achieve highly, some husbands support their wives' accomplishments while others subvert them.

Commitment, Not Quiche

Vandervelde estimates that achiever/obstructionists account for fifty percent of working women's husbands. She originally thought that achiever/facilitators amounted to twenty-five percent of husbands but now believes that this figure may be "very generous." A potentially growing group, she says, is the nonachiever/facilitator (twenty percent), although both the wife and the world may attach a stigma to "marrying down." Vandervelde thinks that only five percent of corporate husbands are nonachiever/obstructionists. As she explained in an interview in the *Wall Street Journal*, "What busy executive needs a man who not only makes less money and has less status than she does, but also is critical of her efforts, disparaging of her associates and unwilling to take household responsibility?"

Psychologists, psychiatrists and individuals themselves agree on the traits that matter to a working wife. "He should be committed to you and to what you're doing," explains Francine S. Hall, Ph.D., professor of organizational behavior at the Whittemore School of Business and Economics at the University of New Hampshire in Durham. "You can buy a quiche or hire a cleaning service, but you can't buy commitment."

Hall, co-author of *The Two-Career Couple*, suggests that a husband should feel successful so that he will be more secure and less competitive. He also should be flexible enough to deal with the ups and downs of daily life. He should share—not just pitch in with—the running of the household: managing finances, caring for children, taking clothes to the cleaners.

Intimacy, Hall emphasizes, is important to a corporate relationship. You should be able to share your feelings and your fears with your husband. While a working woman has to be careful about what she discloses at work, she should feel free to let her hair down at home.

Hall adds that a man should not take a woman's need for her own identity, schedule or "space" as rejection. One 34-year-old unmarried man, a public-sector manager, agrees that a husband must be capable of being alone at times. He expects to marry a woman who is as committed to her career as he is to his and anticipates no drawbacks, only "advantages that far outweigh the fact that she may not be there to cook a meal for me. I'm used to living on my own and expect to share those chores 50-50," he says.

Holding Up The Sky

Not everyone is as sanguine about household sharing. Carol Nadelson, M.D., and Theodore Nadelson, M.D., psychiatrists who practice and teach in Boston, point out that "some men discover late in marriage that they cannot endure the privations of a dual-career marriage; they are too directed toward the comforts that traditional wives can provide. They continue to expect that their wives suddenly will find their places in the kitchen or laundry." A well-placed woman financial executive, who remarried recently, agrees. "Women hold up half the sky until they get married—and then they hold up three-quarters. It's just amazing how many women say that their husbands are involved in a law practice that doesn't allow them to help out at home." The Nadelsons tell the story of two married professors who had similar schedules, statuses and salaries. The wife once turned to her husband and asked him, "In the midst of lecturing to a class, how often do you suddenly think, 'My God, we have no toilet paper!' "

Yet the men who report the greatest sense of well-being in a 1976 large-scale national survey by the Institute for Social Research are those who share, not shirk, household tasks, reports Ronald C. Kessler, Ph.D., assistant professor of sociology at the University of Michigan in Ann Arbor. Kessler thinks that these men's willingness to share domestic responsibilities reflects their ability to adjust and adapt to situations.

What about the charge that working wives are more likely to get divorced than nonworking wives? Hall contends that the stress of a two-career marriage may serve as a catalyst to divorce, but is seldom the cause. Shirley Johnson, Ph.D., chairman of the economics department at Vassar College in Poughkeepsie, New York, has studied the association between women's earnings and the probability of divorce. Johnson says it is a complex issue and that the expectation of a divorce affects the degree of involvement in the labor force. In others words, a woman may try to earn more if she feels her marriage is shaky.

What about the estimated ten percent of two-paycheck families in which wives earn more than their husbands? Carin Rubenstein, Ph.D., a social psychologist and senior editor of *Psychology Today*, interviewed one man who felt his wife's greater earnings afforded him security and a cushion in case something happened. An important determinant of men's reactions, Rubenstein observes, may be whether the salary discrepancy is expected (she is an executive; he is a teacher) or a surprise (she just shot up in sales; he just lost his job). According to Kessler, the more money a wife earns, the better her husband's sense of well-being. Kessler surmises that the increase in buying power provides at least a financial payoff for any personal costs associated with having a working wife.

What Every Woman Should Know

While there are unwritten rules for traditional marriages between a man who works and a woman who does not, modern two-career couples still must "fly by the seat of their pants," concludes David G. Rice, Ph.D., professor of psychiatry at the University of Wisconsin Medical School in Madison. Here are some guidelines to make the most of relationships with two working partners:

• Learn how he feels about successful women he knows, advises Vandervelde. Assess his real needs and desires: Does his interest in an independent woman reflect his wish that she have a career or his hope that she not depend on him? Choose a partner who affirms the importance of work, suggests Rice, who is the author of *Dual-Career Marriage: Conflict and Treatment*.

• Confront and resolve competition. Try not to feel that your spouse's successes occur at your expense. Don't make each sacrifice a test of your relationship ("If you *really* loved me, you'd . . ."). Don't sabotage each other.

• Talk to each other. Don't push small problems under the carpet until they become big ones, advises Sager. Learn to listen to what your spouse really is saying.

• Don't permit business behavior to contaminate your home life. You may have to be tough and calculating at work, says Sager, but you must be open and spontaneous at home.

• Recognize that the two of you may be at different phases. Perhaps he has lost his zest for work just as you have found yours. If you've returned recently to the work force, realize that he may have a hard time adjusting to the change.

• Revise your expectations. Is it vital that he go with you to the company picnic, or do you need his support in more meaningful ways? Remember that he may not want to hear a play-by-play description of your day every evening. One man married to an executive-search consultant once told her, "If I'd wanted to be a headhunter, I would have been one."

• Don't train him to be helpless. Make sure you both know how to operate all your household appliances, for example. Some aeronautical engineers claim they don't know how to load a dishwasher or which buttons to press on a clothes dryer.

• Simplify your lives. Install a second bathroom if the morning rush hour grows too heated and arguments keep erupting. Find a delicatessen or Chinese restaurant that delivers day and night, recommends Pat Koch Thaler, co-author of *Working Couples.*

• Spend time alone with each other. "Only in marriage is sex relegated to midnight," remarks Alexander Levay, M.D., a psychiatrist and prominent sex therapist in New York.

• Consider counseling. If your enjoyment is decreasing, your sexual relationship deteriorating and your arguments increasing, therapy may be in order for you and your husband, says marriage counselor Sager.

21 | POSTPONING LIFE

'm surprised to discover that single women who wouldn't
dream of playing the traditional dating game still play another
kind of "waiting" game. Well past the point when these
women are just beginning their independent lives, they live as
though they're camping out. Paintings, posters and prints—if
purchased at all—lean against walls, unframed and unhung.
For years on end, books remain in cartons or perched on "early-
college style" shelves made of bricks and boards. Mismatched
dishes (reminiscent of cheap Chinese restaurants) cover tables
that have been rescued, no doubt, from relatives' attics and
basements. Cutlery comes from the company cafeteria and
dinner from the local takeout or delicatessen.

Of course, men also exhibit this pattern. One man I know
has a beautiful, one-bedroom apartment, but it's furnished with
a collection of castoffs, including the bedroom set he used as
a boy. His dates always complain after spending a sleepless night
in his narrow bed.

People seem surprised when single women deviate from this
pattern, which merely proves how entrenched, accepted and
even expected it is. A friend of mine has a particularly well-
furnished apartment, complete to the salad bowls, ice buckets
and crystal knickknacks customarily received as wedding
presents. More than one man has walked in and said to her,
accusingly, "I thought you said you hadn't been married."

Another woman bought an obviously expensive fur coat
and wondered why she kept being asked, "Who gave it to you?"
It seems it would have been more "normal" or understandable

for her to have received it as a gift than to have given it to herself.

Still another woman purchased a co-op and spent a small fortune renovating it. Her accountant, lawyer, realtor and contractor all were openly astonished that there was no husband in the picture. When they, and others, asked her why she wanted to buy rather than continue to rent, she patiently reminded them that there were tax advantages to owning.

There is, I think, a reasonable position between conspicuous overconsumption and urban camping. Just because there may be no need or excuse to get sterling-for-twelve, that's no reason *not* to buy stainless-for-four.

I'm not writing, obviously, about struggling students, starving artists or anyone strapped and trapped by inflation, but about single women like myself who are well-paid professionals past the age of 25. And the seeming preference for needlessly Spartan surroundings should not be confused with a 1960s-style disdain for worldly possessions.

A woman I know salvaged a sofa from someone's trash and kept it for several years. Since a cinderblock substituted for its missing leg and an Indian-print bedspread hid its stained and ripped upholstery, I assumed that she didn't care about material things. Belatedly, I discovered she did. The day after announcing her engagement, she bought a beautiful new sofa.

The Waiting Game

The woman's failure to make this purchase earlier reminds me of what sociologist Marcia Millman, Ph.D., described as "living a postponed life." She was referring to the overweight women she studied who, more often than not, had never bought themselves nice winter coats. They were, she learned, unwilling to spend the money until they lost their excess weight.

Young mothers play the waiting game when they defer career dreams until their husbands get established or their children start school. The same postponement oftens pervades the lives of unmarried women. But such "savings" can engender serious costs. Investment opportunities are overlooked. Theater tickets aren't ordered. Vacation trips aren't taken. Holidays aren't celebrated, as if decorating a Christmas tree or lighting a Chanukah menorah requires a marriage license.

Professional possibilities may be allowed to pass by, too. An accomplished, attractive 32-year-old I know often is approached by headhunters who tell her she could be earning more money. They dangle offers in front of her, and she steadfastly refuses to accept a single interview. She admits that she might be willing to make a move if she were married. But she is unwilling now to explore the unknown because, as she puts it, "I just don't have my life together yet," a sad summation of her view of the single state.

The reason such women defer making financial decisions, purchasing houses and cars, and taking important professional steps is that "they may fear that these changes would seem to represent a commitment to being unmarried," write psychiatrists Carol Nadelson, M.D., Malkah Notman, M.D., and Mona Bennett, M.D., in the *American Journal of Psychiatry.* "They might make choices that avoid serious and potentially rewarding career commitments in order to keep relationship 'options' open."

When I was in graduate school, my friends and I always marveled at women we knew who would go off willingly to Asia or Africa for a year of fieldwork when everyone knew they could never "meet anyone" there. Other women, conversely, may have pursued careers in which they had minimal interest—nursing comes to mind for some—but in which marital pickings were reputed to be rich. The danger here is that, like the fat women who were apt to wind up without either the figures they coveted or the coats they wanted, they may miss out on *both* satisfying professional careers and the hypothetical husbands for whom they sacrificed them.

I fear that single women still see themselves as second-class citizens. The inability to make certain purchases or pursue preferred career paths indicates and communicates a deficient sense of self-worth. And, what's worse, lamenting what one lacks without enjoying what one has erodes any existing sense of self-esteem and almost ensures some unhappiness or discontent.

The temporary quality of some single women's possessions and pursuits seems an ill-disguised wish for their single status itself to be short-lived. It is appropriate during school and for awhile thereafter to be able to "fold up your tents," stuff your worldly goods into a Volkswagen and move at a moment's notice, but adolescence shouldn't be allowed to continue forever. No matter what Mother might say, adulthood and "real life" can and should start, irrespective of marriage.

Accepting adult autonomy and the reality that you may not marry does not ensure that you won't. No man I know has refused to marry a woman just because she already owns a co-op, a fur coat or a Cuisinart.

22 | THE TERRIBLE TWENTY-FIVES

A 25-year-old assistant book club editor drips disdain when dealing with authors who haven't written The Great American Novel. But what has the editor published herself? Not a word. And what is the main fare of the book club for which she works? Thirty-one flavors of diet books.

• One December, I wrote to a 25-year-old with whom I do business. The following February, when I followed up by phone, she apologized for not having gotten back to me. In March, when we ran into each other, she seemed embarrassed. I finally heard from her—in the month of June.

• A man I know called to invite a 25-year-old woman for lunch. "Oh, no," she said, switching him to her speaker phone, "I'm much too busy ever to eat lunch."

Like the "terrible twos," from which I've taken the name, the terrible twenty-fives do not befall all 25-year-olds. And, like the terrible twos, the ailment may not begin precisely on schedule. Women as young as 23 and as old as 27 have shown its symptoms.

Although I'm restricting my focus here to women, many men also exhibit this affliction. Men may adopt different affectations, of course. One budding gourmet pulled out a pocket pepper mill in a hamburger hangout and a nascent oenophile went on (and on) about the house wine.

What's behind all these affectations and this brash, brazen—all right—*bad* behavior? A lot of things that happen at once.

At 25, many women are understandably awestruck at the

newness of it all. Perhaps they have toiled away as apprentices or assistants since graduating from college. Or perhaps they have been kept busy (and poor) picking up additional credentials or graduate degrees. Either way, by 25, they are starting to move into responsible roles at work.

Heady Changes

Certain accoutrements accompany such career moves. A young woman may get her first gasoline charge card, car-rental card, air-travel card or even all three. She may be sent across town or, possibly, overseas to entertain or make deals on her own. This is all, unquestionably, heady stuff. But too many 25-year-olds try to overcompensate for their excitement about what's happening in their lives by appearing blasé, accustomed to it all.

Personal changes compound these career changes. They exchange blue jeans for briefcases and grown-up suits—even if doing so means spending their salaries, as well as their Saturdays, shopping. Some seem afraid of appearing to be a fresh-faced "Before," and apply enough makeup to resemble an overdone "After" in a beauty-magazine makeover. But they safely can ignore the ads for acne balms, as well as those for moisturizing creams, poised, as they are, midway between pimples and wrinkles.

Only partly because they look so terrific, these young women attract the attention of men of all ages (25-year-old women might be labeled like many board games, "Suitable for all ages—8 to adult"). Boyish lads the same age compete with 36-year-olds on the way out of their first marriages, not to mention still older men—old enough to be their dads.

So, feeling their oats, these women have a soaring sense of confidence. But at the same time there are disquieting uncertainties. These women may feel far more comfortable discussing what a date's teenage daughter should do with her life than figuring out how to handle their own intelligently.

Hiding Fears

A 24-year-old insurance agent, for instance, is successful enough to get into selling situations that are too complicated for her to manage alone. Only then, instead of before, will she seek help. And rather than show her anxiety or apprehension, she comes across as someone who gets in over her head and then demands to be saved by others.

Such self-doubts clearly clash with fledgling confidence and with the image these women wish to project. Attempting to be assertive, they instead appear to be abrasive or overly aggressive. Arrogance emerges as a substitute for the assurance they desperately desire but do not—cannot—yet feel.

An MBA, new to a company, probably trembles the first time she has to call an executive vice-president. So, trying to be impressive, she asks her secretary to place the call. The tactic backfires when the senior executive picks up her own phone.

Paradoxically, those who are the most accustomed to achieving—as are many of those about whom I'm writing—have the hardest time accepting and admitting their limits. But these women should know that the lacks or gaps they feel they have are perfectly normal, given their level of experience. What wouldn't be normal is to be perfect—a fact too few women can believe. Indeed, I've never heard a boss complain that a young whiz kid or wonder woman asked too many questions—only that she asked too few.

Without this knowledge, many talented young women have trouble asking, even occasionally, for help. They regard it, wrongly, as a sign of stupidity or weakness, and they struggle unnecessarily to maintain the self-sufficiency they think they are supposed to have.

They then may be surprised that showing off their strengths does not always earn the admiration it is intended to. I once sat between a 25-year-old aspiring entrant in a particular field and a 57-year-old woman who was quite well-established in the same field. Not once did I hear the younger woman try to listen to or learn from the older woman. Indeed, she displayed a remarkable insensitivity and never asked a single question. She talked only about herself. Had she tried to express interest— rather than try too hard to seem interesting—she might have made a far better impression.

Regrets Linger

The real question, of course, may be why this phenomenon bothers me so. I have had the feeling of being a "has-been" of late, as I approach my 31st birthday. I spent several months interviewing young achievers for my forthcoming books and became aware, on more than one occasion, that I was regarded as being over the hill. Then my 23-year-old assistant mentioned that she was preparing to take the aptitude test for admission to business school. I started to reminisce about my experience on the same exam "only" eight years earlier. Jennifer pointed out that the test was differnt "in my day," leaving me feeling that I must have taken it by gas lamp. And then I read an adulatory profile—in *The New York Times*, no less—about a woman I knew when I was at Yale University. The trouble was that she wasn't a professor I studied with or a graduate-school classmate, but an undergraduate I had taught.

Once I moved beyond that combination of animosity and envy that often marks relations between people of different ages, I realized there was something else. I'm aware now, in a way that I wasn't then, that what we do at 25 *does* count. It's not like college where one can always take an "incomplete" and expunge a disastrous course from the permanent record. When I remember certain things I said or did way back then, I cringe.

I'd like to spare younger women the possibly lasting or, at least, lingering damage that can result from alienating or antagonizing people they meet. And I'd like them to know, too, that not knowing everything does not mean they know nothing. What bothers me is the regret and remorse of recognition. It's the realization that, only four years ago, I behaved exactly the same way.

23 | TURNING THIRTY

Advertisers—always adept at capitalizing on our fantasies and fears, and at tuning in to demographic trends—have zoomed in on the Big Birthday in a big way. Yet for the women I know and the women I talk to, as well as for myself, the question is not, "Do I look older?" or "Is my life over?" but rather, "Do I have my life in order?"

For the baby boom generation that has enjoyed an almost endless adolescence and postponed adulthood, turning 30 is a signal to begin taking stock in a serious way. The luxury of time to choose or change starts to seem limited. Women know they still can leave teaching, learn French, enter law school, marry, divorce or have a baby after 30—and many do. But the realization that it soon may be "now or never" starts to sink in around the time of turning 30.

A sense of loss may accompany such taking stock. Women past 30 probably can no longer aim for the Van Cliburn piano competition or shoot for the Olympic Games. Moreover, it no longer is enough simply to have potential; one must live up to it. A woman I know burst on the advertising scene a decade ago as a brilliant, 22-year-old beginner. But she has not met anyone's expectations of achievement, least of all her own. This realization has become so painful that she left her firm and the field for a job with less pressure.

Those who have found a secure and fulfilling professional haven in their 20s often feel that they should be settling down personally as well. When friends are changing diapers or planning pregnancies, it can be depressing to realize that you haven't had a date in six weeks, or even if you have, not with anyone you can count on as a dependable dinner partner, let alone a Daddy.

College reunions seem to bring out these issues. As Wendy Wasserstein, the playwright, has observed so well, women with husbands and children who are not working don't want to attend their reunions because they don't have high-powered careers. The ones with high-powered careers but no husbands and children don't want to attend either. Even the anticipation of such ambivalence can serve as a deadline. At my fifth college reunion, a classmate and I pledged that we wouldn't attend our tenth unless we were "at least divorced."

Thirty-year-olds who realize what *hasn't* changed in their lives often find themselves reflecting, examining and re-evaluating. "One of the most common patients to see a psychiatrist in private practice is probably the single woman of about 30 years of age who, although she may complain of anxiety or depression, is also suffering from being single, from a failure to change status," says Richard Rabkin, M.D., in *Strategic Psychotherapy* (Basic Books).

Changing Places

Such reflections may cause a woman to adjust her priorities in life. "A woman who has made a major commitment to marriage and motherhood in her 20s is, to a large extent, bound by these choices," reports Wendy Stewart, Ph.D., in her doctoral dissertation at Columbia University, *A Psychosocial Study of the Formation of the Early Adult Life Structure in Women*. But it is common for such a woman to begin to build a second life structure oriented toward work outside the home, says Stewart.

On the other hand, "Women who have not formed a satisfactory home base by their late 20s tend to feel an increased urgency to stabilize their lives. . . . Women in this study describe feeling like children in their late 20s because they haven't yet married or had a family, even though they have maintained adult responsibilities in their occupations for almost a decade. . . . A marriage made around age 30 is made under considerable time pressure. While love may be no less a factor than in a marrige made at an earlier age, increasing needs for a stable foundation from which to begin childbearing may result in flawed choice," states Stewart.

Despite the very real gains such women have made in the rest of their lives, the pain of their personal lives may loom as a large price tag and lead them to devalue or dismiss the professional side of life. This stems, I think, from the rather rude awakening that their professionalism did not provide the expected insulation or protection from societal and internal pressures to affiliate, to form a family.

Turning 30 need not be a traumatic experience, though. Here are some points to keep in mind as the Big Birthday approaches:

• *Try not to erect your own obstacle course where real barriers do not exist.* When thinking about enrolling in graduate school, for instance, many women say, "But I'll be 34 when I finish," as though that were reason enough not to enter. The true issue is not whether they'll be 34 but whether they'll have that degree when they are.

• *Accept that life proceeds in stages, and don't demand permanence where and when it is inappropriate.* At 30, one friend of mine bewailed her unsettled career. At the time, she was conducting pioneering work as a fellow in pediatric oncology, having already completed a residency at a prestigious children's hospital and graduated from an Ivy League medical school. I pointed out that her career was progressing steadily; it was just that her profession required a longer training period than most others did.

• *Avoid adding to any deprivation you may feel.* The lack of a law degree does not automatically mean that you aren't a worthwhile and productive person. It simply means that you can't practice law. Being single doesn't ensure loneliness and poverty (many married women may be lonelier and poorer than you are). All it has to mean is that you don't have a husband.

• *Focus on what is present, not on what is missing.* Remind yourself of your accomplishments: Maybe you're behind on one part of your agenda but ahead on another.

• *Proceed without procrastinating or postponing, but without a sense of extreme urgency.* Try to make conscious decisions about your future. This is not the time to imitate Scarlett O'Hara by deciding to think about that tomorrow.

• *Take interim steps before you make dramatic changes in your life.* Spend time with some small children before discarding your diaphragm. Try a short computer course before quitting your job to sign up for a master's degree in information systems.

• *Learn to do something you've never quite "found time" to do:* fixing your car or speaking Russian. This will increase your sense of competency and mastery over your own life.

• *Celebrate turning 30.* Sign up for a cruise or a weekend in Bermuda. If your last birthday party was your Sweet 16, throw a small catered supper. Improve your environment (wallpaper the inside of your closets or cover your bedroom walls with fabric) or yourself (join a gym or treat yourself to a facial).

• *Read* Living Contradictions, *by Joanne Michaels (Simon and Schuster), or* The Other Side of Thirty, *by Victoria Pellegrino (Rawson, Wade).* Neither book is an AAA Triptik, but both are reassuring roadmaps. You'll find that wherever you happen to be, there are other women, too.

PART FOUR

Successful Strategies For Overcoming Obstacles

24 | MISTAKE-PROOF JOB INTERVIEWS

Thirty-six-year-old Margaret had been a full-time housewife since her son and daughter were born. Now that her children were in school and inflation was slashing the family income, she decided to return to work. With her husband's support, she arranged for after-school baby-sitting and started looking for a job. After combing the want ads, she updated her résumé, wrote several letters and was finally granted an interview. She ironed her dress the night before, slept fitfully and allowed extra time to arrive for her appointment. Afterward, she wondered when and what the results would be.

After two weeks passed, a form letter arrived. She was told that someone else had been selected from a vast number of qualified applicants. Why hadn't she been hired? she asked herself. What was the reason for the polite rejection letter? Perhaps she might have done a better job of presenting herself.

Margaret happened to be right. She was certainly well-qualified, but she had flubbed the interview. As a matter of fact, experts agree that many otherwise well-qualified candidates actually lose out during job interviews. Employers, employment agency representatives, personnel officers and successful job hunters can readily pinpoint major mistakes women make on job interviews and can tell you how to correct them.

Preparing For The Interview

Before starting to look for a job, decide what you want to do. "Evaluating yourself and your situation is an essential first step," says Maggie Kurtzman, president of Corporate Advisors, Inc., a Miami executive search firm.

Above all, be realistic. Examine the work situation to determine what suits you and your lifestyle. For instance, if you have small children, you probably should eliminate jobs requiring considerable commuting time in favor of positions closer to home.

Also determine which kinds of jobs to seek. Evaluate your talents, education, experience and training. A lot of experience in one post does not automatically qualify you for the next rung up the ladder, says Alba Foreman, manager of office recruitment for McGraw-Hill, Inc., a New York book and magazine publisher. You merely may have done the same thing over and over again, accumulating one year's experience 10 times rather than 10 years' experience.

Realize that years of academic education do not always put you in line for advancement. After working in a library for seven years, Carla went back to college and obtained a B.A. in English literature. She felt that her work experience and degree would advance her career.

She succeeded in obtaining several interviews, but when the interviewer asked her, "What do you see yourself doing in our company?" Carla could only throw the question back at them, "Well, what jobs do you have open for someone with my background?" She should have analyzed various positions in the company and given more thought as to how she might best fit in.

If you review your talents, preference and objectives in advance, you'll be able to plan your answers. When asked, "What are your strengths?" Carla might have said, "Well, I've heard that you're starting a new magazine division. I've taken advanced journalism courses at school and on the job in the periodical division. I think I could offer suggestions that might help your new editorial department."

Plan, too, how to answer the question, "What are your weaknesses?" so that you can mention a "weakness" that won't disqualify you. Instead of saying, "Well, I have a tendency to dwell on details," you might remark, "Even though I'm apt to concentrate on details, I'm able to keep my mind on the big picture."

Rehearse and edit your answers. When responding to the almost inevitable request, "Tell me about yourself," don't start with "Well, I was born in Indiana." Instead, offer recent, job-related information. For example, a woman applying for a job with a school superintendent might say, "For the past five years I've held increasingly important positions at Northern High."

First Impressions Are Important

Even fleeting initial glimpses can lead to lasting opinions. Therefore it's important to dress in a businesslike fashion, even when you're just dashing into the employment agency to fill out a form. When Ruth Kaplan, account executive at Winston Personnel Agency in New York, sees applicants wearing skimpy T-shirts, she worries that they might present themselves poorly when she sends them out on actual interviews.

Apart from underdressing, be careful about *un*dressing, too. Watch out for wrap dresses that have a tendency to unwrap, or skirts slit to show too much leg and thigh. *Over*dressing is in poor taste also. Your Saturday-night or Sunday best are invariably out of place; a job interview is *not* a social occasion.

The paperwork you bring with you, send ahead or complete on the spot should be clean, neat and appropriate. Smudgy photocopies of your résumé, letters weighted down with typewriter correction fluid, and application forms covered with crossouts do not show you to your best advantage.

Think, too, about what those materials are intended to do. When Karen Borack, assistant commissioner of New York City's Department of Consumer Affairs, hires an assistant, she may suggest a few subjects and ask for a sample of the applicant's writing. Borack does so because the job requires writing reports for television, radio and newspapers. She has been surprised, even shocked, by some submissions. "One candidate brought me poetry," she recalls, "when we were looking for someone to write press releases."

Even before you meet your interviewer, you're likely to be greeted by a receptionist. Don't forget, counsels Kaplan, that the receptionist may serve as an unofficial screener. "Her judgment of you," she remarks, "can make a big difference."

Once the actual interview begins, try not to spend too much time on informal chitchat. "Make the first few minutes count," advises Maggie Kurtzman of Corporate Advisors. If you complain about the weather or the car trouble you had on your way over, you're likely to create a negative impression. Once poor first impressions are formed, it's often hard to turn them around to your advantage.

Approaching The Interviewer

Don't try to get too chummy with your interviewer. Many women spend too much time trying to establish a rapport with their interviewer. Even if you both live on the same side of town and are deeply involved with the new school bond issue, don't get sidetracked into a discussion of it. You're being interviewed for a job, not trying to make a new friend.

This is particularly important when the interviewer is another woman. Kaplan is often put off when female applicants remark, "Well, we women..." or, "You know what it's like being a woman in business."

Nor is there any need to (in fact, there's every reason *not* to) go into detail about what is wrong with your present job or your previous boss. Prospective employers are apt to wonder if you'll be difficult to work with and whether you'll "bad-mouth" them, too.

Don't feel that failing to tell all means that you're being untruthful. Resist the temptation to talk about your unhappy divorce or your child's bout with bad colds. But don't become defensive, either, if the interviewer inquires about such matters.

Felicia, a tall, attractive 29-year-old, bristled and balked when an interviewer asked her what her husband did for a living. But since Felicia had already explained that she had moved because her husband's company had transferred him, the interviewer's curiosity was natural and understandable.

Alba Foreman of McGraw-Hill advises against overreacting or overexplaining when asked about personal matters. She points out that you have several choices when an interviewer asks how many children you have and what their ages are. You can call the interviewer up short, but you will probably minimize your chances of getting the job. You can answer directly, but briefly. Or you can diplomatically reply, "I'm not sure how this relates to the job. May I ask why you consider it important?" If the interviewer wonders whether the demands of child care may interfere with your job, you might say, if true, "My children have never caused me to miss a day's work other than my maternity leave." Or, you might reply, "If you're concerned about day-care arrangements, I've already taken care of them."

Try not to appear too jittery or fearful. Some nervousness is normal, of course, but if you find yourself afraid to ask what you need or want to know, you'll only hurt yourself. Some women say, "I'll do anything," instead of stating a specific job objective, because they want to sound cooperative. This response only makes them sound desperate. If you feel you're qualified for a job, say so—you'll only help yourself.

Jill, for example, knew exactly what she wanted to do, but worried about expressing her goals for fear of sounding too ambitious. An experienced newspaper reporter, she knew that she wanted to cover health news. So she told the prospective editor of her interest, adding that she wanted to cover health for the paper's prestigious science section instead of reporting for its style page. Much to her surprise, speaking up got her the job she wanted.

Try not to let the interviewer dominate you. Susan Holland, president of S.R. Holland, Inc., a Chicago search firm specializing in women executives, emphasizes the importance of arming yourself with intelligent questions. If you fail to ask questions about the job, you won't know what your specific duties are. Don't fall into the trap of thinking that such information is none of your business. As Holland points out, "Interviewers will tell you. They're not playing cat-and-mouse games."

Even if you're sure you know what the job entails (perhaps because it's similar to the one you now have), you owe it to yourself to learn about the particular organization. A secretary in a law firm, for instance, may be expected to work overtime when cases heat up. A secretary in an insurance company, on the other hand, can expect to have regular hours.

But don't come on too strong either. Walking in and telling the interviewer what's wrong with the way the position was advertised or the way the company's parking lot is organized isn't the way to prove you're the one to hire, remarks Half of Robert Half, Inc. Assertive behavior is appropriate. Aggressive behavior is only offensive.

Making The Most Of The Interview

Many women still tend to sell themselves short. By avoiding *over*selling themselves and their experience, they only *under*sell themselves. For example, if you rave about your husband's expertise instead of your own, you will inadvertently reinforce the impression that you're far more interested in being a wife than a worker. Also avoid putting yourself down. More than one woman has outlined an impressive record of accomplishments only to add, "Anyone could have done it!" or "It really wasn't much."

• It's entirely appropriate to stress the similarity between the job for which you're applying and those you've held before. Unless you're applying for your very first job, link the examples you use to job situations instead of school or community experience. It's better to point out, for instance, how you cut costs for your present employer than how you raised funds for your church or synagogue.

• Also, don't sell yourself short by being too brief or elliptical. Never let a negative statement stand alone. Follow it with something more positive. For example, don't just say, "No, I never graduated from college." Instead, you might add, "No, I didn't finish my degree because I was offered an intriguing chance to work for the fashion director at our local department store."

• Similarly, it's better to use explicit answers instead of one-word replies. If your interviewer asks whether you're a self-starter, don't simply say "yes" or "no." You might say, "I believe I am. For instance, on my last job I reorganized the research files so they would be more readily accessible to the staff."

• Don't apologize or agonize unnecessarily. Some women are embarrassed when asked about gaps in their work history. Sheila worried for hours when filling out a Federal form; she felt reluctant to indicate that she had been a full-time homemaker for almost eight years. To her relief, she learned that the question had merely been included to detect applicants who had served prison terms.

• Many women also wear themselves out worrying that a former employer may give a bad reference. While some may, lawyers now advise most employers only to confirm the duration of employment and the position held to avoid incurring lawsuits.

• Don't be upset if your schedule limits your availability for interviews. Interviewers prefer candidates who are currently employed and will respect the fact that you can be there only before work, during lunch, after work or on vacation days. That tells them that you won't run off when you work for them, too.

• A final, still-overlooked point: *Show your interest.* Make sure to ask about growth opportunities within the firm, indicating that you're interested in a long-term career. Employers dislike training someone today who won't be there tomorrow. You don't have to say, "When do I start?" but you don't have to play hard-to-get either. Say, "I think I'd like to work here," or something to that effect, suggests Robert Half of the placement firm bearing his name.

If, despite your best efforts, you're not hired, don't despair and don't stop there. Ask, "What other positions might be available in the company?" recommends Kurtzman. By doing so you just may learn about an opening that hasn't yet been advertised.

Do follow up your interview, but "don't batter or badger your contact," recommends Holland. Ask your interviewer to circulate your resume and keep you in mind for future openings. Once you've had an interview that has gone well, you have a permanent leg up with the company. You might spare *them* the wear and tear, as well as the time and cost, of conducting interviews again. For, whatever the economy, employers still have to have good people and hope to hire them with a minimum of hassles and headaches.

25 | HOW TO GET WHAT YOU WANT

Your idea of a negotiator may be an ambassador who specializes in "shuttle diplomacy," rushing back and forth across the seas to conduct eleventh-hour discussions with the heads of foreign governments. Or you may imagine the hard-nosed criminal lawyer who gets clients off scott-free. Both of these people *are* negotiators, but so are the baby-sitters who ask whether you have a color television before agreeing to work for you, and so is the neighbor who becomes a realtor and gets a buyer and seller to finally agree on the price of a house. And so are you.

Negotiation is a valuable and important skill that you can, and do, use every day, whether you realize it or not. Every time you get the repairman to fix the washer today instead of next Thursday, divide weekend chores with your husband or decide which relatives to visit for Christmas, you're "negotiating."

Yet the word "negotiate" frightens many of us. Negotiating certainly can be scary when you're buying your first house, interviewing for a full-time job or entering any new situation where big sums of money are involved. Here are some points to help you overcome those fears and negotiate more successfully in both your daily dealings and in special high-pressure situations.

Be Cordial

If you were to enter the inner sanctum of a prestigious Wall Street law firm when an important multimillion-dollar deal was being discussed, the quiet and camaraderie would probably surprise you. The parties present would most likely be speaking calmly and even cracking jokes every once in a while, not shouting or shaking fists at each other or storming out of the room. And because, in all likelihood, the opposing parties in such a situation will have to face each other over and over again in connection with other deals, they all want to be sure to maintain respect and rapport.

Your negotiations can and should be this congenial, too. Raising your voice, stamping your foot, slamming the door or banging down the telephone receiver are definitely not the tactics to use. Even if the other person shows anger, do not let yourself respond the same way. There's the danger not only that the discussion will escalate into a full-blown argument but that you will get nothing resolved. Rather, keep your wits about you and be persistent in bringing the discussion back to the matter at hand.

In fact, the best technique for beginning a negotiation is to offer a compliment rather than a criticism. For instance, only a few months after the inside of Melanie's new home was painted, her bedroom ceiling started to peel. She mentioned the matter to her contractor, who then came to inspect the damage himself. When Melanie showed it to him, he suggested that it was most probably caused by a leak inside the wall. Melanie told him the pipes inside had been checked, and there was no leak. She went on to say, "Your painters did a nice job, and I would certainly like to recommend your company to my friends, but part of that one bedroom already needs repainting."

Miracle of miracles, he offered to send the painters back the very next day. Had she said, "Your painters did a poor job" or "You must have given them cheap paint"—either or both of which might well have been true—Melanie and her contractor would have wound up arguing heatedly over the cause of the problem, instead of amicably agreeing on its cure.

Be Flexible

Melanie, in the example given above, did another smart

thing. She thought about what her possibilities were and how much she was willing to concede before she talked with the contractor. She knew for certain that she didn't want to have to pay for repainting the room. She also decided that it would be hopeless to ask for a refund of her money. Instead, she decided that she just wanted the job done again. Had the contractor balked at this plan, she would have been ready with a backup proposal that she paint, and he pay. Knowing how to negotiate does not guarantee you'll always get *exactly* what you want, but being prepared with alternate plans will certainly help you get *almost* what you want.

Know What's Negotiable

Many more things may be open to negotiation than you might realize. But too often, fear of being refused or ridiculed keeps people from making reasonable requests.

For instance, in his book, *You Can Negotiate Anything* (Bantam, 1982), Herb Cohen observes that ninety-five percent of hotel and motel guests check out by the time specified on the sign on the door of their rooms, even if it inconveniences them. Last February, Cynthia and Tom went for a short "second honeymoon" in San Juan. Check-out time at their hotel was one o'clock, but their flight wouldn't take off until six. Cynthia wasn't going to let shyness deprive her of a few extra hours in the sun, so she said to the manager, "May I take a moment of your time? Our flight isn't for hours after your customary check-out time. We take so few vacations that I'd hate to lose a minute here. We would be willing to pay the hotel a small extra fee if we could check out at three-thirty instead of one." Much to her surprise and pleasure, the manager replied, "But of course, and no fee is necessary."

It also pays to make some requests that, at first glance, don't always sound reasonable. You may be surprised. Job benefits, for instance, are often more flexible than you might think. When she got her new job, Suzanne was offered generous health-care coverage, but her husband's medical coverage was adequate for her family. She requested—and received—tuition assistance for her college-age children instead.

Related to the problem of not asking at all is the danger of not asking for enough. Low expectations very often lead to low results. For instance, what a person expects to the paid for a job can affect how much she actually is paid. As an experiment, Brenda Major, a psychologist who teaches at the State University of New York at Buffalo, asked 195 management students to pretend they were hiring someone for a particular job. Each student was presented with an application form from a fictitious job-seeker. The interesting result: Given equal qualifications, the higher the salary an applicant requested, the higher the salary that was offered.

Present The Benefits

When trying to sell any plan, the wise woman emphasizes the advantages it offers for the other person. Suppose you would like to change the hours of your part-time job. Instead of working from nine to twelve, you'd like to arrive at ten so that you can see your children off to school in the morning and then leave the office at one. But perhaps this change offers benefits for your employer as well. You could suggest to her, "Mary, I've noticed that when you go to lunch at noon when I leave, there is no one to handle all the incoming calls until you get back. I wouldn't mind covering the phones from noon to one. All I'd have to do differently is come in an hour later in the morning."

Or you might want to join the task force on word processing that your boss is in charge of, but you know he is considering managerial people only. You could try saying, "Joe, I know that this task force is vitally important to you and to our company. It might be an advantage to include someone with hands-on secretarial experience in addition to the managers you're selecting. If you agree, I'd be happy to serve."

Tackle Points One At A Time

You know better than to bombard your boss with multiple requests at once. If you're smart, you don't request a raise on the same day that you ask for an afternoon off. This is worth remembering when you are at home. Let's say that your husband does four things you dislike: He reads the newspaper during breakfast, he watches the news during dinner, he drives too fast and he tends to bring home artichoke hearts and out-of-season asparagus when you asked him to buy just bread and milk. If you mention one item a month for four months, you'll fare a lot better than if you bring up all four objections at once, which will make you seem like a scold, and will irritate your husband.

Create Options

You know you can't persuade a recalcitrant store manager to provide a money-back return for that expensive new silk blouse. Then you might say, "I understand you can't give me cash, so a store credit slip will be fine." In the same way, when your sister in Wichita invites you and your family for Christmas, and you think that the round-trip drive will wear you out before you start a new job, thank her for asking you, explain your reason for refusing, and suggest that she and her family come to you instead. If she says she'd like to visit but is afraid that away from their home and backyard the children will always be underfoot, you might suggest that, between you, you could hire a high-school student to take all the children on daily outings.

Another way to create an option is to grant a concession that the other person would like. Suppose you want your husband to clean out the gutters this weekend rather than next weekend. Instead of setting a deadline (which may strike him as arbitrary or unreasonable), ask him when he expects to complete the job. Tell him, if he can do it this weekend instead, you will cook his favorite meal for dinner or get tickets for the two of you for next Sunday's football game. He may very well say yes.

Stick To The Present

Bringing up ancient history has a way of escalating a calm conversation into an angry argument. Suppose you want to celebrate your next wedding anniversary at an expensive restaurant and your husband thinks it's silly to squander $60 on dinner and would rather eat at home. This is not the time to say, "You were such a skinflint about our last anniversary!" and reopen old wounds. Rather, offer some compromise, maybe dinner at a nice, cozy cafe that will cost half as much.

Minimize Surprises

Plant or presell new ideas so they don't seem to come out of the blue. When a distinguished literary agent has a proposal for a new book, and sets out to sell the book, she leaks a little information about it to a publisher ahead of time. Similarly, Ellie, who used to travel a lot before she married Larry, knew that he wasn't going to be as keen as she on taking a summer vacation overseas. So, in the spring when Ellie's mind began drifting to exotic locales, she brought home books and travel brochures and left them lying around the house where her husband would see them, and perhaps read them. By the time Ellie got around to broaching the subject, Larry's resistance had been lowered, and he was at least willing to consider the possibility of vacationing abroad.

Clarify

In their book *Getting to Yes: Negotiating Agreement Without Giving In* (Penguin, 1983), Roger Fisher and William Ury say that once you clarify your position and ask the other person to clarify his, the supposed dispute may well disappear. For example, suppose you've been writing the copy for a local company's annual report since 1977. At a meeting, the director of publications tells you that she's been talking to another woman about working on this year's report. Before you get all huffy and puffy, ask what this woman's major contribution would be. Perhaps she has a talent for graphic art or is a photographer as well as a rival writer. You might point out that your experience and knowledge of the company after years of writing the report would be an advantage. The two of you might then be asked to team up and do the report together.

Stand Up For Yourself

It's easy to be intimidated when someone says, "But we've always done it this way" or "That's against our policy." It's common to worry about the other person's reaction—even to the point of wanting to appease the other instead of pleasing yourself. And it's easy, too, to overestimate another person's power and to underestimate your own. For instance, fear of being fired keeps many women from suggesting even a minor change in office procedure. But don't forget how hard it can be for the boss to have to find, interview, hire and train a new employee. Remember that things are often more equal than you may be inclined to think.

Try to apply these techniques to your negotiations. As with any other skill—from riding a bicycle to driving a car—you may feel awkward and uncertain at first, but with continued practice, you'll soon feel more comfortable. And, when you expect to be successful, you'll convey the quiet confidence that increases your chances of success.

26 | THE ONE MINUTE MANAGER

A four-hour seminar that would make me a one-minute manager? What sounded like a waste of time—an all-morning session with the authors of *The One Minute Manager*—turned out to be a wise investment.

I walked in late and almost walked out. Four members of the audience were standing in a smoke-filled room while an instructor at the front of the room asked, "How did you *feel* about that?" "Oh no," I thought, "We'll be doing role playing and all the other 'touchy-feely' exercises that make training programs seem like Tupperware parties."

The instructor turned out to be physician and co-author Spencer Johnson, who reminded me of Richard Simmons, the star of the popular TV exercise show. Kenneth Blanchard, a more placid man and the management consultant half of the partnership, soon stepped in. He was more of a storyteller and, thankfully, didn't make us do exercises of either the Johnson or Simmons sort.

The seminar, it turned out, was but another aspect of the publisher's brilliant marketing effort. The slim, costly book bears a sticker comparing it to "a gem—small, expensive and invaluable." Its publication last year was the culmination of an arduous writing process: Hundreds of photocopies of previous drafts were mailed to actual managers to field-test the text. In the process, the authors obtained some of the raves that shamelessly cover the book's inside front and back covers.

The 30 or so other people in the room with me were not there to write about the book or the program, as I had assumed, but to bid on its paperback rights. I suspect that the publisher's efforts to make *The One Minute Manager* stand out from other management books by having the authors explain the concept in person (thus demonstrating the authors' "promotability") upped the bidding by $100,000. (Paperback publishing houses typically pay an advance against royalties—ranging from four figures to seven figures—which the authors, agent and hardback house share.)

Johnson and Blanchard's message is simple, but not simplistic. The authors' premises included the following maxims (which appear at intervals of about one per page):

• People who feel good about themselves produce good results.

• There are no unmotivated people, just unmotivated workers.

• Managers know what they want their people to do, but don't bother to tell them.

• Feedback on results is the best motivator.
managers would put them into practice.

One-minute management has three components: one-minute goal setting, one-minute praising, one-minute reprimands. One-minute goal setting consists of getting supervisor and subordinate to agree on the subordinate's work goals—a vital ingredient of any performance-appraisal system. Blanchard and Johnson suggest limiting and committing each goal to a single sheet of paper so that the manager can read it in less than a minute. Once goals are set, the subordinate should check periodically to see whether she is meeting her goals.

When setting goals, managers should think carefully about how best to meet them. Too often, managers make goals for themselves such as "hold a weekly staff meeting to keep everyone informed." Weekly staff meetings are not bad in themselves (although they do take a lot of time), but they may not be the best way to keep everyone informed (a memo might be better). If the goal were to "solicit staff members' ideas," then the interaction possible in a meeting would make it preferable to a memo.

One-minute praisings rely on a basic principle of behavioral psychology: Catch people doing something right and reward them for it. The authors elaborate on the necessity of praising approximations of good performance before insisting on perfect performance. Their analogy makes their meaning clear: Suppose you want your young daughter to learn to walk. If you wait until she takes perfect strides across the living room before giving her any praise, you probably will have to push her to college in a stroller. But you don't. The first time she struggles to her feet, you probably clap your hands with delight and call her two grandmothers to tell them. The first time she takes a few halting steps, holding on to your hands for dear life, you probably cover her with kisses. Eventually, with all that positive attention, she not only learns to walk but immediately masters running.

One-minute reprimands are misnamed. Spend a half-minute telling a subordinate exactly what she did wrong and let her know how you feel about it. Then spend another half-minute reminding her how you value her, reaffirming that you think well of her, but not of this aspect of her performance.

At the behest of their public-relations agent, the authors took pains to tell me how relevant *The One Minute Manager* is to women managers. They pointed out that some of the managers mentioned in the book—for example, the fictional Ms. Gomez—were women (with Hispanic surnames to boot). The idea to do this came from field-testing the book and is good but gimmicky.

While new managers may be more likely to recognize their need for guidance and, accordingly, more apt to pick up the book, veteran managers need *The One Minute Manager* as much, if not more. A woman who is wrapping up a 30-year career with a Fortune 200 company that, ironically, has been included in business magazine listings of the best-managed companies, says, sadly, that she has yet to see a boss practice the things that Blanchard and Johnson preach.

Should you apply one-minute management? Yes!

27 | YES, YOU CAN SAY NO

You may not have given much thought to saying no since you sat through Mom's lecture about boys, backseats and bedrooms. But *not* saying no can cause countless on-the-job problems. Although some men have difficulty in saying no, women seem to have more trouble. Two cases in point:

Gloria, a fashion designer for a small sportswear house, felt uncomfortable disciplining a designer who reported to her. Instead of rejecting the junior designer's sketches, Gloria would say nothing and then rework them herself. As a result, her department often missed deadlines and delayed production. When heads rolled, it was Gloria—not her subordinate—who received the pink slip.

Eleanor was a popular speaker who accepted scores of requests from friends of friends to talk (virtually gratis) before their "pet" groups. Then, when she received more lucrative or prestigious lecture invitations, she found she was so over-scheduled that she had to turn them down—thus missing the ones she would have preferred.

The professional consequences of saying yes when you really should say no can be serious, and this practice also carries a stiff personal price tag. Those who seldom say no when they should will find their self-respect shrinking and their resentment growing. Such behavior can lead to a sense of being exploited (often, with reason). Ultimately, suggests Herbert Fensterheim, Ph.D., clinical associate professor of psychology at Cornell University Medical College in New York, the result of not saying no can be depression.

Good Little Girls

Nothing so complicated as an inability to make negative statements can have a single cause, of course. But part of the problem often is that, as children seeking adults' approval, women learned that "good little girls" didn't disagree. As a consequence, Fensterheim suspects, they may not have learned to exercise their right to say no.

To make another person comfortable, many women succumb to what might be called the hostess syndrome. Just as hostesses proffer second and third helpings, some managers are likely to offer too many concessions, explains Roger Fisher, professor of law at Harvard University and co-author, with William Ury, of *Getting to Yes: Negotiating Agreement Without Giving In*. An example might be sacrificing your own client's interests or being too free with your company's money in order to please or appease the other person. Many women are afraid that unless they always play "Ms. Nice Guy" they will make people angry, lack approval and lose affection.

In addition to favoring compliance—even at the cost of competence—women also tend to confuse an interpersonal relationship with an issue being discussed. It's important to remember that relationships with colleagues and clients can be cordial without being close. Instead of worrying, "Will she still like me?" or wondering, "Will he get angry?" concentrate on "Will the job get done?" suggests Fensterheim.

Practice Makes Perfect

Arguing over positions by taking a series of stands resembles a ritualized dance, says Fisher, who directs the Harvard Negotiation Project and participated in the hostage negotiations between the U.S. and Iran. In contrast to other writers on winning what you want, he and Ury advise looking for the common interests that underlie both positions when trying to resolve a discussion. Even opposing positions, they find, often include compatible interests among the conflicting ones. An architect, for instance, may favor windows facing east to allow for morning light while her clients wants them on the west to permit afternoon sun, but the common element is that they both want light.

When trying to reconcile divergent interests, don't fall into the trap of passing judgment on each of them. Instead, act as though you've already accepted them. If you understand the other person's point of view rather than dismiss it out of hand, you may hit upon another strategy that will be mutually acceptable. A supervisor, for example, might have to concede that the union won't allow bringing in temporary workers but instead will permit offering overtime to finish a rush job.

Remember to separate the problem from the people. Fisher discusses refusing a request without rejecting the person who makes it. Thank the person even though you are turning down her request. You might want to say, for example, "No, I won't be able to make it. You're kind to ask me. I'm flattered but can't accept."

Fensterheim, who also writes extensively and has a private practice in behavior therapy, agrees. He suggests depersonalizing business decisions. You might pretend, for instance, that you are teaching an MBA course and that the situation you are facing is a question on an exam. Ask yourself what would be the best business answer your students could give.

Fensterheim also suggests that you practice saying no. It may sound simpleminded, but rehearsing and reviewing your own behavior often yields good results. Talk into a tape recorder and play back what you say, trying out different versions to see which one is best. Be sure to start off with the word *no* so that your response doesn't wind up as a weak *maybe* or even a *yes*. Be brief to avoid any tendency to become apologetic. Use a strong, firm speaking voice so that you don't sound as though you really want to be persuaded or convinced to change your mind.

Try not to retreat into passive ploys, such as having someone else say no for you, procrastinating or saying "I'll get back to you" when you have no intention of doing so.

Saying no in novel situations may make you feel anxious, guilty or uncomfortable the first few times. Relaxing and focusing on what you've accomplished by saying no may help you overcome such feelings. Some discomfort accompanies most new behaviors, and most likely it will disappear with practice.

28 | DEALING WITH DIFFICULT WORKERS

According to a management cliché, "There are no problem people, only people problems." But there may be moments when you disagree.

• Ellie hasn't been on time once since you hired her and, come to think of it, she was late even then.

• Paul's work has been worthless since his divorce.

• The two secretaries who sit outside your door seem to squabble nonstop from 9 to 5.

What can a manager do in these situations? First, don't assume that every difficult worker has psychological problems. "Troubled employees are not always troubling employees, and troubling employees are not always troubled," cautions Robert M. Bramson, Ph.D., senior partner in Bramson, Parlette and Associates, a Berkeley, California, management-consulting firm.

You may not have the information or the training to tell whether an employee is psychologically troubled or merely troubling. In either case, though, the manager can do something about the situation. Signs of trouble can include increased absence or lateness, accidents or illness, an upsurge in personal phone calls, a decline in appearance, frequent requests for advances on salary, avoidance of usual customer contact and other undesirable changes. "You're not interested in behavior that's an exception to the rule, but in behavior that's beginning to establish new rules," says Patricia G. Abelson, MSW, director of employee-counseling programs for the Jewish Board of Family and Children's Services in New York. Adds Marilyn Puder, Ph.D., assistant vice-president in charge of staff advisory services at Citibank in New York, "If a person comes in late, don't assume she's an alcoholic."

Since wishing won't make a problem go away, don't delay taking action. If you do something when a previously terrific worker first shows signs of sliding, you may be able to prevent her from becoming a terrible worker. "A supervisor should never cover up or ignore the warning signs," says Puder.

Don't be tempted to play "shrink" either: Coaching is part of a manager's role, but counseling is not. Even if you have professional training in counseling, the neutrality necessary to be an effective counselor is incompatible with supervisory responsibilities. "I've seen more trouble occur," explains Bramson, "when supervisors who took a supervisory counseling course got 'hooked' on doing too much counseling."

Performance, not attitude. Before interceding, establish standards for an employee's acceptable performance. Define these standards in ways that can be observed and measured: arriving on time, meeting printers' deadlines, making the requisite number of "cold" calls, achieving production goals and so on. Investigate your company's policies and procedures regarding discipline and dismissal, in case the employee's performance doesn't improve. Plan, too, how you will approach the subordinate and initiate the discussion—this task is too difficult to think that you can simply "wing it," notes Bramson.

When you talk to a troubled employee, emphasize performance rather than attitude, advises Bernard L. Rosenbaum, Ed.D., president of MOHR Development, Inc., a Stamford, Connecticut, consulting firm. Employees' attitudes often are invisible and even irrelevant, Rosenbaum explains in his book, so it can be counterproductive to concentrate on them. If you allow the conversation to drift to the person's motivation and personality, you may increase her defensiveness, denial, rationalization, passivity and aggressiveness, he explains. "A productive discussion of performance problems," Rosenbaum writes, "will focus on the problem, not on the employee, and will concentrate on the future and the solution, as opposed to the past and the cause."

Ask for the employee's help in resolving the situation. As you listen to her suggestions, be sure to indicate that you understand what she says (even if you don't agree). Clarify what you don't understand and communicate your understanding so that she knows she's getting through to you, Rosenbaum advises. To make sure that you, in turn, are reaching the employee, look for signs that she is paying attention. It's a better sign if she gives many excuses rather than a shrug of indifference, says Bramson.

Sympathy isn't the answer. Agree on the steps to be taken by each of you and set a follow-up date to review progress, recommends Rosenbaum. Indicate the consequences—for example, termination—of failing to improve. Express your confidence in the employee's ability to correct the problem— citing previous examples of successful effort, if possible. Praise her at the first small sign of improvement.

While this approach may sound harsh, it may be crueler to overlook poor performance out of a misguided sense of sympathy. Most managers allow a little leeway when a worker's child gets sick or parent dies, but permitting deficiencies to become chronic helps no one, states Bramson. People take pride in work well done, observes Abelson, and they know when they're not performing well. Accepting poor performance as a norm may make it legitimate not only for that person but for others in her work group, adds Puder.

When you are unable to solve the problem or when the employee indicates that the problem lies outside the workplace, you may want to consult personnel specialists in your company for training and guidance. If an employee-counseling program, such as New York's Citibank's exists on-site, it would be a service and not a slap in the face if you suggest that the employee talk to a counselor.

Such facilities originally were formed to focus on the three A's of alcoholism, absenteeism and accidents, but today corporate psychiatrists, psychologists and social workers tend to hear more about such problems of daily life as debt and divorce. Such services still are controversial in some quarters, but most are careful about maintaining confidentiality and overcoming potential conflicts of interest when they are serving the individual at the expense of the organization.

Off-site services, such as Abelson's (which serves employees of Xerox, Exxon and other corporations and unions) are another referral resource. If neither type of service is available at your company, suggest that the employee see someone in the personnel or medical department who is familiar with community resources.

One advantage of psychotherapists working in occupational mental health is that they may be more sensitive to organizational politics and procedures than the typical psychotherapist. Then, too, adds Abelson, the traditional psychotherapist may interpret a worker's reluctance to accept a 3:00 p.m. appointment as resistance to treatment rather than a reality of the workplace.

29 | REVIEWING THE TROOPS

Performance appraisals—formal, periodic evaluations of an employee's work—are becoming more and more common, and important, in corporate life. In theory, they usually are meant to review a subordinate's progress objectively and to identify areas that need improving. In practice, they often influence career advancement and salary increases.

Yet despite their importance and impact, performance appraisals remain something of a mystery to both supervisors *and* subordinates. Some supervisors are confused or troubled by rating procedures. Performance-appraisal forms usually require a supervisor to write a summary of a subordinate's work to date, rank her against other employees in the division, rate her on a wide array of qualities or match her accomplishments against previously-stated objectives. Some bosses don't feel comfortable about sitting in judgment, evaluating behavior that they haven't observed adequately or simply saying, "You really haven't performed well."

Subordinates, on the other hand, may have a poor idea of the standards by which they're being measured. Then, too, they may be so intent on hearing "the bottom line"—the size of their salary increase—that they ignore all other information pertaining to their on-the-job performance. Or they may become defensive at the first sign of criticism and thus discourage further feedback.

Some of these problems can be solved easily. Hiring consulting firms to train managers in conducting sensitive performance discussions seems to make managers more confident;

as a result, they become more competent. Revising rating scales and systems can simplify and standardize evaluation of performance. This helps avoid the situation in which one manager interprets a score either more leniently or more stringently than another—some managers tend to reserve "outstanding" for God, "superior" for themselves, and "adequate" for everyone else.

No secrets. Still, other problems in giving—and receiving—performance appraisals persist. Some of these may not be directly related to the performance appraisal itself but may point to flaws in a company's procedures in other areas. Poorly defined jobs and unclear job objectives, for instance, can render useless even the most effective rating form. An employee's objections to the way his or her performance is evaluated, actually may reflect a company's poor communication with employees or difficulties in its pay policy, says Martin Greller, a consultant in New York with the Chicago-based consulting firm of Rohrer, Hibler and Replogle.

Fortunately, suggestions and solutions abound. A supervisor and a new employee should agree on what the employee's job entails, which aspects will be evaluated and what constitutes unacceptable, acceptable and excellent performance, counsels Darlene Orlov, president of Orlov Resources for Business in New York. "If you set these goals together," she adds, "you get commitment."

Orlov advises conducting performance reviews at midpoints between salary reviews: Employees must perceive a performance appraisal as separate from a salary review. Otherwise, contends Orlov, they will disregard the performance feedback and just concentrate on the "dollars" under discussion.

At this time, too, Orlov suggests, it would be both valuable and appropriate to show your subordinate how she can improve before the next salary review to warrant receiving the maximum increase. "If you keep that a secret for 12 months, it really isn't productive. Your employee won't know what's wrong in time to improve." When the official performance-appraisal period occurs, your feedback won't come as a shock if you've been appraising performance all along.

Hard facts. During a review, supervisors should try to use objective information wherever possible. Such statements as "Achieved sales quotas" or "Cut departmental costs" are easier to evaluate and substantiate than opinions such as "Displayed good attitude." Supervisors might benefit from keeping a written record of a subordinate's performance between appraisal times, says Edward E. Lawler, Ph.D., professor of organizational behavior at the University of Southern California.

When the time for performance appraisals comes up, supervisors should not delay them. Postponing an appraisal or canceling it may suggest a lack of concern, poor preparation or disregard for the subordinate, explains Orlov.

Subordinates are not exempt from preparation, either. Orlov suggests that new employees obtain a copy of the rating form as soon as they start their jobs. Then they should ask their superior which aspects of their performance will be measured and by what criteria. They should substantiate their accomplishments, saving copies of work, photocopying complimentary memos, listing awards received and presentations made, and so on. From time to time between appraisal periods, they might ask the boss for pointers.

And while supervisors should initiate performance reviews themselves, don't count on them to do so. As Orlov concedes, "Some supervisors are like clams." An employee should be prepared to ask for an appraisal.

30 | SPEAKING OUT

B esides being a lucrative sideline for a lucky few (fees range from a few hundred dollars to $15,000 per speech), public speaking is one of the best ways to boost a career. "The exposure you get by speaking is one of the most effective ways to become a recognized authority in your field," says Sandy Linver, president of Speakeasy, Inc., an Atlanta consulting firm, and author of the book *Speak Easy.*

Before you get started, though, there's a lot to learn. Judith Marcus of Communication Dynamics, in White Plains, New York, emphasizes the following skills: (1) Analyzing the audience—who is there and why? (2) Defining the objective— what do you want people to get from your speech? (3) Structuring the story—getting your audience's attention, proper pacing, making connections between ideas, a forceful conclusion. (4) Designing the visual aids—will you give handouts before the speech? Afterward? Will you show slides? How will you handle these details? (5) Establishing eye contact and control—how will you deal with questions and answers? At the end, or interspersed? How will you handle a heckler? (6) Projecting the voice. (7) Using stance and gesture.

Getting started. Sign up for a speaking course. Companies, colleges and consulting concerns offer them. (Jacqueline Thompson's *Directory of Personal Image Consultants*, Editorial Services Co., lists quite a few.) Make sure the course you select uses videotape training. Watching yourself lean to the left, hop from foot to foot, or twist your watch is a cruel but quick way to learn which habits need changing. As painful as it can be to view yourself for the first time, you will notice remarkable improvement by the second or third time.

Plan what you'll say. Speak into tape recorder to maintain your conversational tone, suggests Linver. Then, write a detailed outline or a few large cue cards. Talking from a word-by-word text can sound stilted.

Practice, practice, practice. Enlist a small child, your spouse, a colleague, a friend, a mirror or a tape recorder.

Edit mercilessly. Delete phrases that trip you up or examples you'll never remember. Humor is fine, but jokes belong in Las Vegas. Don't respond to flowery introductions—as too many speakers do—by saying, "My father would have loved it and my mother would have believed it." Do leave room for local or topical references, where possible.

Consider your setting and circumstances. What may work at a brown-bag luncheon may be too informal for a 400-person audience in an auditorium. Seventeen slides and a synchronized soundtrack may be fine when you have professional assistance, but may be hard to handle on your own. Plan for contingencies: What will you do if the handouts you prepared are lost in transit?

Before going big-time, make sure your presentation suits a larger audience than your company or your industry. Try it out a few times and, if possible, secure letters of thanks that compliment you on your talk. Then contact lecture bureaus, which are listed in Bowker's *Literary Marketplace* in your library. For a commission (usually thirty percent) these agencies will promote your availability, book dates, make travel arrangements, collect fees, and provide a variety of other services. The time and travel needed for an extensive speaking schedule can be a plus or a minus, depending on your perspective. Other possible perks include invitations to speak on luxury cruises or at posh health spas.

But, be warned: Your expertise may not be much in demand. On the lecture circuit, executives are far outnumbered by consultants, authors, athletes, politicians, professors, critics, pollsters, comedians and newscasters.

31 | GAINING VISIBILITY

Good managers know the value of visibility. Janet Wikler, director of electronic publishing for the Times Mirror Company in New York, is a case in point. Wikler studied English and elementary education and worked for ten years before she decided to go to business school. By mastering a hot field—the new technologies and their application to the publishing industry—she was able to land jobs in organizations that needed her high-tech expertise and so were willing to catapult her up. "Any time you have a skill that is in demand," she explains, "you increase your visibility and thus your marketability." Wikler also built up a network of peers in the industry, got on task forces and participated in trade associations. Her strategy has paid off in better jobs and higher salaries.

Indeed, in the upper reaches of management, the promotions of highly-visible people regularly attest to the value of keeping a high profile. A recruiter hears or reads of you frequently and then automatically thinks of you when an appropriate position comes her way. Or a chief executive officer runs into you so often at charitable, civic or professional functions that your name heads the list when she wants to add a new director to her board.

Promote Yourself

Visibility means displaying and magnifying your accomplishments and yourself. There are many ways to make yourself more visible, but don't try to exploit all of them at one time. Select one or two ideas from the list below, according to your own style and your industry's culture. Forget about instant results; the benefits of visibility accrue over time.

Do a good job. "The best visibility you can get is to write big tickets," claims Robin Krasny, MBA, a fixed-income securities broker for a Wall Street investment firm. "Your sales figures are no secret," says Krasny, whose performance has won her training and travel opportunities.

While competence alone can be enough to attract attention in divisions or positions that focus on the bottom line, sheer technical proficiency may not be recognized adequately in staff capacities. So do a good job—but don't stop there.

Look the part. The image industry has taken pains to teach us that appearance plays a part in hiring and promotion. But as lone women in male settings have learned, this way of standing out may not always work in a woman's favor. Wendy J. Robins was working at suburban Detroit television station while she was preganant. "As my shape changed, so did my image," she told *Business Week.* "Instead of being the assistant producer, I was Wendy Robins, pregnant lady."

You will have to take pains to preserve your credibility when your appearance changes because of pregnancy or other reasons, such as a dramatic weight loss. Maternity warrants the risk, but frequent changes of hairstyle or color probably do not.

Get out there. Writing and speaking are obvious ways to become better known in the business world. They even can help you in your own company. Carol Kleiman had been a features writer for the *Chicago Tribune* for 12 years before her book, *Women's Networks* was published. Although Kleiman had been under the noses of the *Tribune's* financial editors for years, it was only after her book came out that they offered her a coveted spot in the business section.

You may not have the time or talent to write a book, but you can contribute an article to your house organ, trade-association magazine or local newspaper. It is perfectly suitable to route copies of such pieces, with a brief cover note: "Thought you'd be interested."

Join. Headhunters and reporters often refer to the membership directories of professional societies. Kleiman regularly flips through the roster of the Chicago Network, Inc., a prestigious group of working women, when seeking sources for her articles. She jokes that she hardly needs the Chicago phone book.

You might want to volunteer for the program committee of your professional association so that you have the opportunity to host prominent speakers. Even time-pressed executives find that being an officer of these associations can pay off. For one thing, their names are on the association's monthly mailings that often go to hundreds of members.

Even if you don't aspire to leadership in your professional association, you still can make your membership work for you. By inviting a senior executive from your firm to join you at a meeting, you may give her a new view of you. You'll also have a chance to interact informally with her out of the office. Both of these points can be positive for your career.

Cut across levels. While you want to catch the eye of those above you, remember the value of lateral or even downward visibility. Pay attention to people—particularly young whiz kids—who cannot help you today but may be in a position to do so later. I recently attended a meeting at which Henry Kissinger was the premier attraction. While many people clamored for his attention at the coffee breaks and cocktail hours, wiser attendees chatted with less-renowned participants.

Remember that you're always on display. Be careful about what you say in bathrooms and elevators—someone whose good opinion you value may be listening. After an unsatisfactory meeting with a potential client, two businesswomen stopped in the bathroom on their way home. In the safety of the bathroom, the two women compared their unflattering views of the potential client. But the women soon discovered they were not alone—the potential client also was in the bathroom and had heard their criticism.

Tackle tough assignments. Top executives probably pay more attention to trouble spots in a business than to smoothly running operations. If you solve problems or turn losing operations into profit centers, you'll attract their notice, too.

Bring your work out into the open. Even if a report or memorandum does not bear your name, you can make your role known. If you talk up your project during lunch and take the floor during meetings, your co-workers will know who really did the work.

Be modest. When extolling your role, don't grab all the credit. Donna Ecton, the president of MBA Resources, one of the nation's ten largest executive recruiters, advises that you learn "to brag humbly." Don't blow your own horn when you can talk about the entire band. If you say, "My team pulled in seven new accounts," people will get the point that you had something to do with it.

No matter how tactful you are about increasing your visibility, you may be charged with being a publicity hound or a self-promoter. Expect criticism but don't let it deter you, unless, of course, you have been overdoing your campaign.

Reposition yourself at career junctures. If you are promoted and you behave exactly as you did in the past, you will be treated as you used to be. If you know that your superior is going to step aside or your sidekick is about to leave, be ready to move into their spots. You might quietly assume their role—acting as company spokesperson at a press conference, for instance. Once the change is public, you might mail announcements of it.

Modify your routines. Many managers plop themselves down first thing in the morning and communicate by phone instead of picking themselves up and walking around. Dropping in on people or delivering items in person may not be the most efficient use of your time, but they're easy ways to help people attach your face to your name and to remind them that you're there.

Extend your reach outside your company, too. Instead of

having lunch with the same threesome every day, try to meet your peers at other companies. If geography stands in your way, you'll have to be innovative. A firm with which I've worked is located just far enough from Boston to make it inconvenient for people who work downtown to come to the firm for lunch. To get around the problem, one women who lives in Boston started meeting her counterparts in town for breakfast at a posh hotel, before driving to her job. She thus avoided making a round trip to Boston at lunchtime.

Low Profiles

Some obstacles to increasing your visibility can crop up. Certain occupations, for instance, have built-in barriers to visibility. Joyce Newman is president of Newman & Nolan Communications, a speech-writing and coaching service in New York that is part of the Betsy Nolan Group. Some of her clients are at the top of their fields and are reluctant to admit they need her help.

Like anyone with a behind-the-scenes role, Newman exercises discretion. She asks companies' permission before she lists their names in her promotional literature, and she never lists the names of individual clients. She does ask each individual for a letter to show to prospective clients on a limited basis.

Some companies deliberately try to keep low profile, and this may impede your efforts at developing an independent image. The law firm that frowns on publicity for itself, for instance, will not look kindly on the lawyer whose name appears in the newspaper. And, even if your firm does maintain a high profile, it may reserve public roles for staff members who outrank you. Should the limelight fall on you, be prepared for reproving comments (often in the form of kidding).

You will have to decide whether visibility is a help or a hindrance. You may have to channel personal publicity so that it does not offend your firm. If you decide that your long-term future lies outside your firm, you may want to go ahead with your plans to become more visible so that other companies will recruit you.

The advice in this chapter may seem calculating; it even may strike some women as cheating. But it is up to you to orchestrate the course of your own career, and to do so means making sure that you and your work are visible.

32 | INSIDE MOVES

An internal transfer—changing jobs within your company—can be a smart career move. Internal transfers expose you to new areas of your company's operations, add to your expertise and so hasten your upward climb. They take you out of dying departments and put you into developing ones; they get you out of such sticky situations as working for a boss you can't stand; and they save you from launching an exhausting job search and starting over at a new company where you wouldn't have the vacation and other fringe benefits you've accumulated over the years at your old company.

You may be able to get a better job inside your current company than you could outside. Diane Felmlee, Ph.D., a sociologist at Indiana University in Bloomington, studied 3,500 women and the job changes they made. Felmlee found that women got better, more prestigious jobs by making internal transfers than by switching companies. The reason? When you and your work are know quantities, your lack of such credentials as an MBA may be overlooked. Seniority and on-the-job performance count more. When you're applying from outside a company, education or experience requirements can serve as barriers.

Appealing as they are, internal transfers do entail risks. If the new slot doesn't work out and your old position already has been filled, you may be demoted of dismissed, cautions Kay Wallace, president of Operations Improvement, Inc., a management consulting firm in St. Louis and author of *You're the Boss* (Contemporary Books). If your new department has been hit hard by budget cuts, your contribution may be limited from the start, Wallace adds.

The attitude of staff members in your new department also may stand in your way. If your job is a common steppingstone, subordinates who are tired of managers just passing through may not work with you; they simply will wait you out, explains Jeanne Brett, Ph.D., associate professor at the Kellogg Graduate School of Management at Northwestern University in Evanston, Illinois.

Some in-house transfers may mean relocation. If the division to which you transfer is in another city or state, you will face the normal adjustment problems, and the sacrifices of your ·move may lower your job satisfaction for awhile. Brett studied mobile managers who had made many transfers, most of them requiring relocation, and stable mangers who had stayed put. She found that stable managers were more satisfied with the opportunities for growth than their migratory co-workers. She hypothesizes that mobile managers expected more from their companies in exchange for their move and that their elevated expectations were not always met.

Shirley LaPiana had risen to be a product manager for mustard at R.T. French Company, a food-manufacturing firm headquartered in Rochester, New York. Two years ago, LaPiana was asked if she would consider becoming personnel manager for the Rochester operation. LaPiana thought hard about moving from a line to staff role, since line jobs often mean greater earnings and recognition. And, LaPiana points out, "In any consumer packaged-goods company, marketing is perceived to be 'where it's at.' " But LaPiana accepted the personnel position because general management is her goal and she believed that a broadening move might help her rise.

Some women have taken internal transfers to change their specializations. One woman had gone far in the human-resources department of her company, but she was curious about computers. After investigating the field, she decided to take a significant demotion and pay cut to enter her company's data-processing division. Several years later, she has caught up to her previous level and is much more satisfied with her job.

Another woman completed law school at night while working as a secretary for a large financial-services organization. She thought of seeking a legal job elsewhere but hesitated because her degree was not from a top-tier school. Since her reputation at her current company was good and her pension was almost vested, she transferred to her company's legal department.

Not all transfers work out so well. One sales-support specialist for a large company had many fallings out with her boss, and their relationship had reached an impasse. She wanted to get out of his department at once, so she accepted the only available position at her level. Unfortunately, her new job turned out to be even worse than her previous position, bad boss and all. Should she seek another transfer, superiors may conclude that she, not her bosses, is the cause of her problems.

The Risks And Rewards

To make the most of an inside move, here are a few guidelines.

• *Assess your company's climate.* If top management truly is committed to promoting from within, transfers can help you advance, says Darlene Orlov, president of her management-consulting firm in New York. Examine the careers of top execs to see what moves they made, Orlov suggests. Follow the paths of managers who have transferred recently to see how their careers develop. Before accepting any assignment, try to find out what happened to your predecessors. Figure out, too, whether you can decline a transfer safely. Learn whether a sizable number of people are seeking transfers *from* a particular area—a sure sign that something's amiss—or *to* any area—a sign that opportunities may exist there.

• *Go to grow.* New profit centers provide ideal opportunities. When your company reorganizes or carves out a new department, you can reap all of the rewards of getting in on the ground floor, with few of the risks of joining a new venture. A woman who worked in traditional publications department transferred to her company's new electronic-publishing group. She now has more subscriber contact and better future prospects.

• *Exercise political skill.* During almost 13 years with one employer, Karen Fraser, director of executive development for CIGNA Corporation in Hartford, Connecticut, has zigzagged her way toward senior management. (CIGNA is the insurance firm that was formed when Fraser's original employer, Connecticut General Insurance Corporation, merged with the Insurance Company of North America last year.) Fraser started in data processing and moved to human resources. Another inside move took her to marketing, and yet another brought her back to human resources. Fraser managed to increase her salary and her responsibility with each move.

Surviving and thriving while learning to navigate a complex corporate structure have become second nature to Fraser, and she has this advice for women who transfer: Learn how your company perceives your potential and performance through some careful, candid conversations with your superiors. Make sure, adds Fraser, that you understand the personality, power structure, philosophy and politics of the organization. As with any new job, be aware of covert expectations, suggests Wallace, the St. Louis consultant. Does management want you to make changes or keep thing on course?

• *Use both formal and informal channels.* When Laurie Hutton was a staff analyst in the installation-and-repair department of Southwestern Bell in St. Louis, she cultivated some contacts she had made at company meetings and told them that she'd be open to a change. The payoff? Hutton is now corporate communications manager at American Telephone and Telegraph Company (AT&T), Southwestern Bell's parent company, in Piscataway, New Jersey. Adding contacts in other divisions— particularly personnel—to your network may bring opportunities your way.

The higher you go, the more you must supplement formal programs such as career banks with informal personal contacts. A clerical worker can apply for many of the positions publicized through a job-posting system, but you can't afford to become known as someone who bids on every opening. In any case, job listings are shams in some companies: A front runner often has the inside track, and posting the opening is merely a formality.

• *Learn whether to involve your boss.* Ask an experienced co-worker about the etiquette of bypassing your boss. Hutton proceeded on her own until she needed her boss' signature on the official forms releasing her from one department to another. Another woman, by contrast, knew that her boss wanted her to grow and could suggest strategies, so she involved her boss from the start.

• *Know your goals.* A lateral change that involves no increase in responsibility or pay may be worthwhile if you want to leave a terrible situation or if you want to become a generalist. Otherwise, cautions Wallace, beware of horizontal moves that don't add to your pool of skills.

• *Expect an adjustment period.* Even though the company is the same, the job may be completely different. Both old and new co-workers may be puzzled by your move at first. When LaPiana left marketing at R.T. French, her friends wondered whether she had been demoted and didn't know whether to congratulate her or commiserate with her. When Hutton joined AT&T, her new co-workers couldn't understand why she was qualified to make the move until they learned of her earlier related work. Consider whether your personal life can withstand the stress of a move. If not, suggests CIGNA's Fraser, consider postponing the change.

• *Continue working.* Trying to change jobs can be a full-time job. Do not allow your performance in your present job to slide. Your track record is the most important asset you have in making an internal transfer, says Fraser.

The open-mindedness and imagination you develop in considering an internal transfer is an ability itself. It will help you whether you make such a move now, later or never at all.

33 | YOUR COACHING COMMITMENT

Developing subordinates is one of those important, basic functions of a manager that is so obvious it can get taken for granted. Such fashionable concepts as "mentor mania" distract our attention from the much more common work relationship of supervisor/subordinate. Relatively few people are or have mentors, while almost all of us are or have supervisors. Developing subordinates is a critical component in promoting from within to ensure organizational succession, perpetuation and regeneration. New studies by three Boston behavioral scientists tell us how good managers can fulfill many of the multiple functions of mentors for the subordinates they are developing and why they should.

"The majority of people don't have mentors," explains Kathy Kram, Ph.D., an assistant professor at Boston University School of Management, who studied developmental relationships among employees of a public utility. "The focus on mentors has tended to discount the value of other relationships, with superiors and even peers. Looking for one person to carry you throughout your career can lead to chronic disappointment."

"Young people early in their careers seem intent on finding a mentor to smooth the way for them," concurs James G. Clawson, DBA, an assistant professor at Harvard Business School who researched superior-subordinate interactions at a large insurance company. "The belief that everyone must have a mentor can be dangerous and counterproductive. It can usurp a lot of time and energy that could be channeled more productively."

Clawson, like Kram, advocates relying on different people

to help them develop both professionally and personally. "A young person embarking on a new career may have relationships with one individual who will take an interest in teaching technical skills, another person who will outline the political realities of an organization, another who will push senior management for promotion, another who is willing to discuss world affairs and yet another who is willing to listen to and give advice on personal matters."

There is a lot to learn whenever you enter a new organization. Harry Levinson, Ph.D., president of The Levinson Institute (a consulting firm in Cambridge, Massachusetts) and lecturer at Harvard Medical School, lists the most important information a newcomer to the work place needs to know:

1. where the power in the organization is and who has it;

2. what the norms, standards, values, ideology, history and heroes of the organization are;

3. the skills and competencies necessary to succeed and advance;

4. the paths to advancement and the blind alleys;

5. acceptable modes of visibility;

6. the characteristic stumbling blocks and personal failure patterns.

No one sponsor or superior could provide all of this information and, furthermore, the consensus of information from several sources is apt to be more accurate than any single set of answers.

Clawson says the first boss in a person's career may be particularly important. He or she is the one who introduces the new employee into "the way we do things around here." The ideal superior for this role needs to be a strong developer of subordinates or, at least, someone who can structure early contact for the new employee with such developers. The only way to ensure that this happens within a department is to incorporate subordinate development as a criterion for promotion and as a part of every performance appraisal. "Unless senior manage ment really holds people's feet to the fire on subordinate development," concedes Clawson, "it falls by the wayside."

When Clawson and Edward H. Nelson of Business Development Services, Inc., a Fairfield, Connecticut, consulting firm, teach managers how to coach their subordinates, they work on both their attitudes and their behavior. They encourage managers to explore their own attitudes about the quality of relationships with subordinates. Frequently, for instance, managers think that they must maintain distance in order to make hard decisions about a subordinate's ability or to give negative feedback on performance. Actually, according to Clawson's research, the most effective developmental relationships are characterized by being "close but not too close" and frequent interactions—meeting two to three times per day.

Clawson and Nelson also teach managers how people learn. "People learn from a variety of sources: other people, books, mass media, experience, schools, etc. These sources compete with one another. Managers are always teaching their subordinates something (even how *not* to manage). Every interaction has an additional impact on a subordinate. People learn when they are open to learning. People learn at different rates, at rates consistent with their own abilities and openness. People learn what they are rewarded for."

Clawson and Nelson also teach how to pick up covert communication from subordinates and how to foster more overt communications. Both of these entail listening carefully "without," Clawson cautions, "seeming phony and put on." (That "what-I-hear-you-saying-is" stuff.)

It is important that the superior makes the subordinate's work visible in various ways—through presentations, reports over her or his signature and so on. Developing subordinates requires a commitment; it is an ongoing interaction—not a one-shot action.

Sex differences still affect superior-subordinate relationships. It is up to both parties to make sure that others in the organization understand the nature of their relationship. They can achieve this by including others in their discussions and meetings so that their colleagues can pick up the clues that signal that the relationship is not a sexual one and can draw their own assessments of the subordinate's capabilities.

Seek the counsel of senior management and other people's opinions when making promotion decisions; this will help to avert scurrilous comments. Solo sponsorship can lead to a precarious position.

The parties involved in this kind of male/female relationship must sacrifice a certain amount of casualness, notes Clawson. While a superior and subordinate of the same sex may blithely continue a discussion over dinner, a pair of the opposite sex might be better advised to stick to lunches. Similarly, while no one might think anything about two men or two women leaving the building together late at night or walking through the parking lot together early in the morning, a man and a woman have to pay more attention to appearances. What Clawson calls "audience judgments" are one of the constraints for managers.

34 | MANAGING CONFLICT

Today's successful executive must be a mediator and conciliator, bringing together disparate viewpoints to move (her) organization forward," says Gerard Roche, chairman of Heidrick & Struggles, a New York-based executive-recruiting firm. Although many executives would agree that the diplomatic skills of Philip Habib are essential in the corporate world, they admit they've never studied mediation or other formal means of resolving conflict.

Their ignorance has high costs. Conflict can destroy a good working relationship, as "issues give way to personalities, parties become polarized, and problems get fuzzy," explains consultant Thomas L. Quick, author of *The Persuasive Manager*. Even after employees have forgotten what the initial dispute was about, they may persist in opposing their former adversaries to justify their original stance, says Jeffrey Z. Rubin, Ph.D., professor of psychology at Tufts University in Medford, Massachusetts. To prevent new conflicts from igniting and old conflicts from flaring, psychologists recommend the simple techniques outlined here.

Cooling Teapot Tempests

There are two basic approaches to resolving conflict. The first is to act procedurally by charting responsibilities, clarifying job descriptions, citing regulations or establishing operations standards. Or you may prefer to proceed personally by negotiating the dispute yourself or calling in a third party to mediate.

With either approach, the first step is to gather all the facts. You need to define or perhaps redefine the problem to clarify the underlying issues. Otherwise, even illusory conflicts can become a reality. To overcome tunnel vision, you also should test your perceptions of the problem with someone else.

When Meg Jones (not her real name), a manager at a north-eastern computer firm, received an unusually formal, negative memo from her boss, she resisted her first inclination to panic and confront him angrily. Instead she asked other members of the department if they had received similar notices. They had. She then tried to learn whether her boss was up against any professional or personal pressures. As it happened, he was in hot water with his own boss. She concluded that her boss had written the annoying note to protect himself from rumblings higher up the office hierarchy and that she simply should hold her tongue and wait. Jones confided her problem to a close friend, who confirmed her interpretation of the memo and assured her that no action was necessary. Nothing ever came of the negative memo and Jones realized that she had been wise to remain silent.

After gathering background information, the second step should be to scan your options. In Jones' case, no immediate action was indicated. In most cases, though, you should address a problem as early as possible. If you put off dealing with a disagreement, it can grow. When my clients reach an explosion point and exclaim that they are ready to "tell someone off," I suggest they simply tell the other person what is bothering them, before they have to tell him or her off.

Rachel Green (not her real name) learned that the best way to handle conflict is by anticipating it, developing possible solutions and then talking dispassionately about them. Green, manager of a six-person data-processing department, believed her group needed a second secretary. Rather than storming into her boss' office and demanding a new secretary, Green first asked her staff to report on projects that couldn't be completed because of a shortage of support services. She then checked on her superior's budget limitations and deadlines. Using all this information, Green documented her department's predicament and outlined a solution. She presented her plan to her boss in plenty of time for budget review and discussed it with him in detail. By making allies out of both her subordinates and her superiors, Green managed to win approval for her budget request.

Once you've drawn up a list of options, you must choose and use a strategy. In Green's case, one plan of action seemed obvious, so Green did not consider other possibilities. The choices sometimes are more complex, though. Weigh their probable outcomes and costs.

The director of a research and development laboratory, for example, learned that she was going to lose some of her space as part of a political ploy to satisfy managers who envied her empire. She considered confronting her boss, or alerting the product managers who awaited the results of her research. She decided to tell the project managers that experiments would be canceled if there was no room for her crew or equipment. The project managers interceded on her behalf and she kept her space, without alienating her boss.

Unlike nations, managers sometimes can't afford to follow a policy of noninterference when conflicts erupt. If members of your staff are at war, you must mediate if their disputes threaten to disrupt the office. The presence of a third party speeds resolution, explains Rubin, the Tufts professor, because opposing parties don't feel they're losing face when a neutral party suggests concessions. Be careful about jumping into conflicts between staff members, though. If you dictate a solution—by telling two support-staff people how to keep the supply room stocked, for example—you may become the scapegoat when the system breaks down.

Try to mediate instead by getting the parties to reach a solution themselves. Mary Rowe, Ph.D., special assistant to the president of the Massachusetts Institute of Technology (MIT) in Cambridge, functions as an ombudswoman or internal mediator. Rowe will either talk to all parties involved in a conflict or with the one party who visits her, depending on the visitor's wishes and the gravity of the conflict. For example, if an employee claimed a supervisor hit her, Rowe would intervene immediately. Generally, though, Rowe prefers to help the party settle the dispute by herself.

Rowe listens sympathetically as the aggrieved party talks to her. After letting the person talk as long as necessary, Rowe asks the person to present the opponent's probable response to this complaint. "Most people are extremely good and very fair at doing this," Rowe finds. Finally, Rowe asks what actions the offended person would like to take. These actions range from forgetting the incident to filing a formal grievance. The person usually takes a middle course and decides to handle the matter herself or himself.

Rowe willingly stages discussions in which she plays the aggrieved party's opponent. She also is amenable to reading a draft of a letter the person might wish to send but prefers that she not be given a copy of it or listed as someone receiving a carbon copy. Unlike Rubin, Rowe thinks that "public exposure (of her role) is not necessarily the most effective course." She believes that it is more important that the person take the responsibility for solving problems and win credit for so doing.

Rowe uses the same technique for conflicts over allocations of money or objects. In these cases, she finds that each side typically possesses different data or perceives the same data differently, so that the clarification a neutral party provides often can resolve the dispute.

Final Pointers

• Keep any discussion on track by being as specific as possible about the grievance, advises Hyler Bracey, Ph.D., president of the Atlanta Consulting Group, a management-consulting firm. Check periodically for understanding, Bracey adds. If an employee is complaining that her rank entitles her to use only the general cafeteria, not the executive dining room, determine whether she is requesting a promotion or searching for a way to entertain clients at lunch. Knowing which issue is at stake will affect how you proceed.

• Focus on performance, not personalities. A manager in the Southwest bypassed a subordinate for a promotion and hired an outsider. The thwarted subordinate refused to work with the newcomer and made angry accusations. When speaking to the subordinate, the manager concentrated on the consequences of not meeting job objectives and did not get pulled into a personality clash.

• Realize that conflict can be beneficial. A young woman who was an account supervisor at an ad agency in Kansas City, Missouri, regards conflict as "evolutionary rather than disruptive." When developing an ad campaign, agency staff discuss (often heatedly) different approaches until everyone is convinced that the campaign the agency presents to the client is the best one. As she explains, "If you sound the least bit unsure or the agency staff doesn't seem to support the plan wholeheartedly, the client picks that up very quickly and will be more likely to kill the campaign."

• Decide which issues are negotiable and which are not. "Sometimes it isn't feasible to do exactly what the client wants," acknowledges Susan Warner, owner of Cinema Associates, a communications-consulting firm in Arden, Delaware. Warner has passed up assignments that would have meant sacrificing her professional standards.

• Remember to go back a step when resolution eludes you. Seek new facts or explanations or try new techniques or tactics. Rowe, the MIT mediator, "never gives up" on resolving a dispute and is willing to sit down with the parties again six months or two years later.

Running away from conflict only can hurt you. Airing conflicts, on the other hand, can lead to creative, cost-effective solutions to pressing business problems. Uncomfortable as conflicts can be, confronting and resolving them is more effective in the long run than silently trying to sail along.

35 | DANGER: WORKAHOLIC AT WORK

Workaholics are easy to identify. Take the advertising executive whose office is almost unfurnished because "anybody who has time to sit down doesn't have enough to do"; the bank officer who continues to work after her husband goes to bed and who sleeps only three and a half hours a night; the entrepreneur who locates her company in an apartment so that employees who stay late can shower; or the chief executive officer of a computer firm who sends out her electronic mail at midnight.

Working for a workaholic can be delightful or disastrous. Nancy Trachtenberg, vice-president of Richard Weiner, Inc., a New York public-relations firm, has a number of workaholics among her clients. Working with them, she says, has given her many years of experience in just a short time. Trachtenberg finds their work styles invigorating and inspiring—"You don't want to let them down."

Trachtenberg probably is satisfied, though, because she is a workaholic herself. By contrast, other employees believe that workaholics misuse them. Jack Falvey, a management consultant in Londonderry, New Hampshire, claims that workaholics "don't want managers working for them—they want machines."

To a workaholic, everything is a number one priority. This exaggerated sense of urgency can create a constant state of emergency and disrupt planning. Also, because the workaholic focuses on her own goals, she may mistake her priorities for those of the organization.

The pressure to perform that workaholics (as well as other

high-powered managers) put on others can backfire. Research directors have been held responsible for medical data falsified by their pressured subordinates, creating not only scandals but false hope for the sick and futile leads for fellow scientists.

Workaholics may not be as efficient as they seem. They may sacrifice reflection for action and proceed at full speed in an ill-advised direction. It is easy to mistake being busy for being productive.

Finally, more than peace of mind is at stake if you work for a workaholic. The misuse that Falvey identifies can become abuse. If workaholics do not delegate—or if they oversee every detail when they do—they discourage their subordinates from learning and advancing. One workaholic executive treats her senior managers as though they were worthless lackeys, over-ruling their initiatives and allowing them little autonomy. Some subordinates, doubting their own abilities, stay put. Others leave but find themselves ill-equipped to handle unaccustomed responsibility at their new firms.

If You Work For One

Learn the workaholic's language so that you can decipher her demands. When she says, "I'd like to see this soon," does she mean your report is due next Tuesday or today? Don't accept a deadline you know you can't meet. Discuss the deadline first so that you won't have to request an extension later. Try to separate artificial deadlines from real ones. You may need to make an ally of the the workaholic's assistant to determine whether the date for a report really has been moved up ten days.

Address the issue of different standards of dedication before you start the job. Is working on Saturdays an unwritten part of your job description? If you aren't willing to put in more than the 40-hour weekly minimum, the job may not be for you. But your unwillingness to work 80-hour weeks does not mean you are lazy. When you discuss your hours, concentrate on what you are willing to do. Offer to come in early rather than simply stating that you refuse to stay late, for instance.

Work apart, when possible. When Falvey and a workaholic boss both traveled a lot, he tried to make sure that they wouldn't be in town at the same time. It might be possible to suggest tactfully that you stagger your schedules or work at home one or two days a week, without making it obvious that you are trying to avoid working too closely with your boss.

Above all, you have to decide whether you will be able to work with a workaholic, because you won't be able to change her. Try to ascertain whether her work style is only a temporary response to a current crunch or is part of a lifelong pattern. You don't need to ask her directly; instead, ask those who have worked with her longer. Offer to assume part of the work load when she is either reluctant or too mistrustful to delegate responsibility.

If You Are One

Remember that, as a woman, you will be judged more harshly than a man with similar habits and drive. Don't apologize for your ambition. Acknowledge your expectations and make them explicit. Don't pretend the day stops at 5:00 p.m. if you often work later, advises Richard Keller, president of Viceroy Imports, Inc., a wine and spirits importer in Ramsey, New Jersey. Keller, who has worked with both men and women workaholics, frankly tells job applicants that his staff "spent Christmas Eve last year preparing a marketing plan."

Respect the private lives of your subordinates. Are you more mindful of the word processor than the man or woman behind it? There are no hard-and-fast rules about how much time you can expect subordinates to devote to their jobs. Still, there are some rules of thumb: If you expect the excessive demands to be chronic, consider adding to your staff. If the peak periods will be only occasional, try to give employees as much advance notice as possible to assist them in their planning. Remember that the sacrifices you're willing to make when you earn $75,000 a year may seem too high to a subordinate who makes only $25,000. When you staff puts in a heroic overtime effort, acknowledge and reward it.

Give your staff freedom. Don't peer over their shoulders—literally or figuratively. And don't keep important information secret; tell them what they need to know to get their jobs done. One workaholic client of mine shares sensitive statistics with his entire organization. He asks only that they remember that "nothing is secret, but everything is confidential." His trust has not been betrayed.

Don't overschedule yourself. Leave longer gaps between appointments, or cluster all meetings in the afternoons to leave your mornings free. Learn to say no. Don't become the victim of upward delegation—on the whole, you can refuse to read subordinates' drafts and turn down continual requests to provide direction. Do the parts of your job that you like or do best—chances are, they're the same—and delegate the rest.

Resist the temptation to take attendance (for example, by noting who is at her desk earliest). It's more important—and harder—to measure performance. Put staff planning and appraisal sessions on your calendar or do them during a retreat in order to force yourself to perform this valuable exercise.

The inveterate workaholic should hire only in her own image. I have read Help Wanted ads that began "Workaholic Wanted." This approach can work even if you're not a workaholic. Many managers who wouldn't want to work for a workaholic say they certainly would like to have one work for them.

36| VELVET GHETTO?

Once a dumping ground for "good-ol'-Charlie who can't cut it anymore in marketing," human resources departments (née Personnel) have achieved new status in most corporations. They now are attracting well-qualified men and women with MBAs, Ph.D.s and JDs.

Salaries reflect this new status. Most human resources professionals now are on a par with their counterparts in other staff departments (support units such as advertising and purchasing). In the largest organizations, the top human resources executive often earns $150,000, and can even top $200,000.

The new role of human resources departments has stemmed, in large part, from government regulation and legislation. While equal employment is expected to receive less emphasis in the 1980s, the human resources field is expected to continue gaining in stature. Sixty-nine percent of top managers and 73 percent of human resources managers surveyed by the Opinion Research Corporation of Princeton, New Jersey, expect the importance of the human resources function to increase in the next five years. (Only 1 percent of each group believes that the status of human resources will decline in the near future.)

Women traditionally have done well in human resources departments. But are these positions a route to the very top executive jobs in a company? The answer: rarely.

"If you look at male executives," says Pearl Meyer, executive consultant of Handy Associates, an executive compensation, search and consulting firm in New York, "a very small percentage have become chief executive officers after a career limited to human resources." She notes that line jobs in marketing, finance and operations still are more likely paths to power. She doubts that this pattern will be different for women on the way up.

Women face one additional obstacle when it comes to careers in human resources. While many are appointed to high human resources positions, quite a few of these appointments are made purely for window dressing. Madelyn Jennings, senior vice-president for personnel and administration at the Gannett Company, Inc. in Rochester, New York, acknowledges that human resources remains "one of the functions in which it has been easier for women to succeed." Others grudgingly agree that some human resources departments still are "velvet ghettos" full of females in plush, well-paid, but almost powerless positions. But Mary Jean Wolf, staff vice-president for personnel and compensation at Trans-World Airlines in New York, contends that able women entering human resources departments *can* get things done even if they were intended to be only figureheads.

Activist role. Alert to the pitfalls of winding up in an human resources department where policy-making is precluded, Jennings, Wolf and other leading women in human resources distinguish the old-style departments from such powerful ones as their own. Jennings, for instance, is a member of Gannett's Office of the Chief Executive, indicating, she says, that the company recognized that "the 'people function' needed to be part and parcel of policy-making." Wolf considers it imperative to "determine a department's style." She contrasts administrative departments bogged down under piles of paper with activist, innovative "hands-on" ones.

Betty A. Duval, vice-president for staff development at Dow Jones & Company, Inc. in New York, encourages examining the "breadth and depth of personnel programs and activities." But as soon as she had spoken, Duval corrected herself. "It's not just 'Personnel.' Today we think of the work as human resources management. 'Personnel,' in the classical sense, was a control-oriented organization that dealt with the records— the administration of programs—rather than tried to under- stand the needs of organizations in their business goals and the needs of individuals and groups in their personal and career goals." She continues, " 'Personnel' looked at programs as separate entities" (rather than as a total system with interaction among the programs). Personnel "didn't recognize the changing environment in which business works and in which people live."

The impact of the changes in human resources departments is something Duval feels and faces daily. As her own company looks at and expands into such areas as electronic publishing, Duval and her colleagues on the management committee must concentrate on developing or recruiting the managers such new ventures require. She also must be aware of changes in employees' needs and values. To do so, Duval leaves her well- appointed offices and serves on the copy desk, accompanies delivery people on their 4:00 a.m. rounds and visits production plants and news bureaus around the country. Through these opportunities to observe (as well as more traditional meetings), Duval has learned, for example, that some salespeople wondered whether their expense accounts might allow taking customers to health clubs instead of restaurants.

These top women in human resources also emphasize the personal and professional experiences needed to prepare for advancement within the human resources field. Most agree that beginning in human resources instead of a line function can limit a career later on. Jennings advises women to gain experience and early exposure in line functions. "Too often," she observes, "people have only been in personnel." She recommends that a recent graduate in, say, industrial relations, start in a sales or supervisory spot and not in recruiting or employee relations.

Jennings also advocates getting training in labor relations, a key area from which women often are excluded. Wolf agrees. Her stint as manager of labor relations in the New York region —a position in which she handled grievances and administered labor agreements for John F. Kennedy, LaGuardia and Newark airports—contributed greatly, she says, to her growth. It taught her to see both sides of any argument, placed her in innumerable adversary situations (where someone or one side was always unhappy) and increased her independence because it "forced me to learn to stand alone."

37 | CORPORATE TRAINING – BOOM OR BUST?

Trainers have been working behind the scenes in corporations for years. They design, develop and teach courses in subjects as varied as typing and advanced management. They select films and workshops by outside training companies, recruit experts to teach in-house, and choose outside courses in which to enroll company employees. These days, though, corporate training departments are attracting a lot of attention, especially from women in the public sector who eye them as points of entry to a business career. Teachers who make the transition stand to double their salaries when they become trainers.

As the pace of technological change quickens, many companies view corporate trainers as key players who help coordinate human resources with strategic business plans. Such companies recognize that today's work force must be trained and retrained in tomorrow's technology. Other companies, however, regard these departments as nonessential frills, and they can be hit hard by cutbacks.

Career Boost Or Dead End?

Women in training departments may face even more serious problems than possible cutbacks in budgets or personnel. These departments are, in fact, full of women whose power is limited; they are "velvet ghettos." Even women who enter these departments directly from college or graduate school with degrees in Personnel don't necessarily get ahead much faster than those who transfer from other careers.

Whatever a woman's background, men move up more rapidly within training departments than do women. One such man is Raymond Ivey, who taught for 12 years before becoming a trainer and supervisor in a management-consulting firm. Ivey wanted to see whether "I could transfer my skills to the business arena."

He could and did. Five years ago, Ivey moved to CBS Inc.'s small training department in New York. He now is director of education and training there, and his department has grown significantly since he started. Ivey's career path is identical to that of many women who enter the field, but, while he suspects that the situation is changing, he consedes that "unfortunately, men appear to rise more quickly to the top."

Even women at the pinnacle of the training hierarchy echo Ivey's—the higher you go, the fewer you see, explains Bettye Baldwin, vice-president of human resources for Home Life Insurance Company in New York.

Line vs. Staff

Even if women (or men) rise in training departments, they are unlikely to move up in the corporation unless they have broader experience. "There isn't too much movement out of training," observes Bonita Perry, Ph.D., former director of Sun Institute, the training and development arm of the Sun Company, an oil concern in Radnor, Pennsylvania.

Why is this so? Perry, who now runs her own marketing-research business in Philadelphia, explains that trainers may not be interested in or suited for more technical aspects of their companies' operations, like chemical engineering. She adds that they may be pigeonholed as trainers and passed over for other moves they are qualified to make.

A recent survey of members of the International Association of Personnel Women sought to determine what differentiated those women who were on a fast track from those who proceeded more slowly or not at all. The results showed that the fast-track women (those who had been promoted three or more times in the preceding five years) held technical roles (such as compensation and human resources information systems) rather than service or welfare positions. According to the survey, "The likelihood of . . . failing to advance is greatest for women who have responsibilities in such areas as education, counseling, career development, communications, and training and development."

Then, too, there is the customary tension between such line functions as manufacturing and such staff ones as training. "Training and development are not preceived as powerful functions by line operating people," says Roberta Jones, president of the Jones Group, Inc., a recruitment firm in Hasbrouck Heights, New Jersey. Baldwin takes care to remind trainers that they must serve the line and not their own intellectual interests. As she puts it, "Home Life is not in the human-resources business, it's in the life-insurance business."

Those already in training should understand the business of their companies by obtaining some hands-on experience rather than just learning the lingo. Gaining credibility with petroleum engineers is hard if you've never seen an oil rig, points out Katherine Beal, vice-president of manpower and career planning for Barclay's Bank International in New York. Learning the business also helps in designing training programs that replicate actual jobs. Otherwise, you run the risk of having a trainee shout, "We haven't sold the product in three years," says one expert.

A line manager can sabotage training by failing to enroll her staff or by pulling people out of a program at the last minute, If a trainer establishes a relationship with the line manager, however, her chances of success will increase, says Perry. Line managers may undermine training for other reasons as well, explains Salvatore Didato, Ph.D., a management consultant in New York. They may feel that their departments' out put will decline while workers are attending training sessions and that this will create more work for them, he continues. They also may think that training their own staff is *their* job, he adds.

Involving managers in the training process not only cuts their resistance but improves the program. Perry recommends including some line people—perhaps those nearing retirement—to avoid allowing the pool of trainers to grow stagnant. Encouraging outstanding supervisors and the program. "A training organization shouldn't be made up of one hundred percent trainers or of one hundred percent line people," cautions Baldwin.

Criteria For Success

Trainers must know the skills that the company will require three to five years years down the road, says Beal, so that they can identify opportunities for retraining. Beal explains that retraining is necessary when technology changes, jobs become redundant or procedures are updated. The danger in not tying training to the strategic plan and corporate goals is that a trainer will "wake up with a work force that can do one thing and a company that's going in another direction," Baldwin asserts. Because retraining programs can be expensive. Alma Baron, Ph.D., professor of management at the University of Wisconsin-Extension in Madison, Wisconsin, advocates organizing them on an industry-wide basis.

Personal qualities can determine your success as a trainer. Training requires patience—it may be years between the time a course is conceived and actually conducted. Many courses may never even get the go-ahead. Training also requires enthusiasm. Dealing with the concerns and questions of yet another crop of recruits can be boring and draining. To avert burnout, Perry recommends restricting tenure as a stand-up trainer to three to five years. "After that," she explains, "you need to get your own batteries recharged."

Breaking In

Perry urges prospective trainers to join organizations where training receives adequate financial support, sufficient staffing and top-management attention. For example, at Sun, Perry had a $1.1 million budget, a staff of 16 and a chief executive officer who addressed training sessions. Top-management support means high-level reporting relationships for the head of training and, Perry found, "sets the tone for the rest of the company."

Once you're in a training department, seek out the hottest, most technical areas. Perry recommends a career in retraining because it requires "retooling people" when "traditionally, training was fine-tuning people."

As a next step, she recommends moving up the ladder in your organization or joining a smaller company where your duties will be more diversified. To make the tough move from training into a line function, align yourself with some of the departments whose personnel you train. Doing a bang-up job— and letting your goals be known—may get you a new assignment.

Another option for you to consider is starting an independent training business yourself or joining an established training company, such as the Forum Corporation of North America, Xerox Learning Systems or Wilson Learning Corporation.

The advantage of joining a training company, adds Perry, is that training can be a line rather than a staff function. Financial rewards can follow. While entry-level corporate trainers earn $17,000 a year, seasoned management-development people in corporations earn around $45,000 and top people in corporations earn about $75,000, according to Al Pleasanton, president of Pleasanton HRD Recruitment Inc., which specializes in Personnel. Training company employees eventually can earn much more than this.

The conclusion to be drawn from all this? While corporate training departments are not an expressway to the chief executive officers spot, neither are they always a dead end. Corporate trainers muct create their own opportunities and always try to tie their efforts to a corporation's bottom line.

PART FIVE

The Last Word

38 | STOP PUTTING YOURSELF DOWN

Lynn hates her thighs. Every summer she says she won't go to the beach until someone designs "a floor-length bathing suit." All Lynn's friends think she is an attractive woman with a nice figure. They never noticed her "figure flaw," but now they can't forget it—Lynn won't let them.

Donna went all out planning a birthday party for her eight-year-old daughter. She hired a clown, ordered the cake and invited 18 of her daughter's friends. But on the big day, a snowstorm prevented the guests and even the clown from attending. Donna's daughter *was* disappointed, but Donna was miserable, blaming herself for the weather.

Just two weeks after her promotion, Mary told a friend she wanted to return to her former position, because "I can't seem to get everything done. I'm not sure of my new responsibilities." What Mary may be overlooking is that it takes *everyone* a few months to get on top of a new job.

The Guilt Trap

Like many women, Lynn, Donna and Mary are all victims of their own self-abuse. Part of their problem is perspective: When the flaws and faults are our own, we tend to view them as larger than life. We assume, as Lynn did, that they are written on our foreheads for all to see. Realistically, we know this isn't so.

Women also tend to assume responsibility for events beyond their control. While, logically, we know we have no control over the weather or other unexpected events, many of us do what Donna did: We blame ourselves, agonize and apologize anyway.

Some people, such as Mary, expect too much, too soon. By choosing unrealistic goals for ourselves, we're setting ourselves up for failure, and when we do fail, we may end up feeling worthless. The more we do this, the worse our opinion of ourselves becomes.

Accentuate The Positive

Many women feed themselves messages and myths about their shortcomings—statements that focus on "mistakes" they have made, are making and will make. Yet even the most successful people have had their share of mistakes and near-misses which we often don't know about because most autobiographies just highlight the successes. For instance, before founding Neiman-Marcus, the famous Dallas department store, the Marcus family passed up the chance to invest in a soft drink operation that was just getting off the ground. Fortunately, the department store prospered and grew to a national chain. But the soda company didn't do badly either. Its name? Coca-Cola.

When Isaac Asimov, Ph.D., wrote his first book of science fiction, a friend advised him to stick to academic science and forget about fiction. Heeding that early critic could have been the biggest mistake of Dr. Asimov's career! He went on to write more than 260 books (so far) and to become spectacularly successful as a writer rather than as a scientist.

It's important to remember that most mistakes aren't disastrous. Many are reversible, as long as you haven't burned your bridges behind you. One woman once worked for an Oregon department store chain but left to pursue greener pastures. Well, apparently the grass didn't stay greener, so she returned to her former employer. Her current title? President.

If you acknowledge your mistakes and disappointments you're less likely to repeat them. Learn to scrutinize the early warning signs of the problem so you'll be better able to prevent it. And most of all, trust your instincts. Listen to your inner voice when it tells you, "Watch out, this situation is a lot like the last one."

When you *do* make an honest-to-goodness mistake, rather than focusing on the problem, concentrate on the solution— what you can do to correct or minimize the damage.

• *Remember, nobody's perfect.* Examine your assumptions about your own behavior. Perhaps you think a person should be "nice" all the time. When you realize that no mortal can do this, you might change your expectations. Revise your view to the more reasonable: "I should be nice when appropriate." And then you might make your view even more specific: "I should be nice to my mother-in-law when she visits." That way, your standard for yourself will be more possible to achieve.

• *Describe yourself positively.* Many of the statements you make—even privately—do yourself a disservice. For instance, when I hired my first employee, I made many mistakes supervising her: Sometimes I was too strict and sometimes I was too lenient. I concluded that I was simply a bad manager. I confided my conclusion to a friend, who corrected me. "No," she said, "you're just an *inexperienced* manager." I felt much better and was able to improve my supervisory style.

• *Stop scolding yourself.* If you give yourself a pat-on-the-back for sticking to your diet, you will be less tempted to raid the refrigerator than if you say, "Oh, I'm so fat, it won't matter if I cheat anyway."

• *Accept both your peak and slow phases.* You can't operate at full speed all the time. You need that time to evaluate your priorities and recharge your energies.

For example, if you have a baby less than three months old—and neither she nor you are sleeping through the night—don't even attempt to throw a fancy dinner party. Save that for later. Similarly, when your office is in the middle of a crunch, you should feel free to devote extra energy there, even if it means letting things slide a little at home.

• *Make time for yourself.* Many working mothers are so

reluctant to shortchange either their employers or their families that they wind up shortchanging themselves. They rush home from work to be with the family, when what they may need most right then is to be alone.

Build in some transition time at the end of the working day. This may simply mean sitting in your car to read the paper in peace, before entering the house. Or it may mean joining an exercise club. This isn't selfish, it's sane. This technique may make you less irritable and more available to your family when you do walk in the door. You'll be doing both yourself and your family a favor.

• *Update your self-image.* Remind yourself that you're a serious woman now, even if you used to be a frivolous girl. You have to take yourself seriously before anybody else will. "When I look around the workplace," Betty Rollin, an ABC television correspondent, wrote in *The New York Times,* "I see an awful lot of men who are less competent than they think they are, and as many women who are far more competent than they know."

• *Take pride in your accomplishments.* Don't minimize them or attribute your successes to "dumb luck." Research by Kay Deaux, Ph.D., a professor of psychology at Purdue University in West Lafayette, Indiana, suggests that women are far more likely than men to explain achievements in this way. A female singer, for instance, may attribute her skill to a terrific teacher, rather than to her own talent. A career woman might tell you that she just happened to be "in the right place at the right time" and overlook all the years of hard work she put in.

Regardless of the evidence that supports their talents or hard efforts, these women think that they've simply slid by. The price for this self-defeating thinking includes anxiety, limited enjoyment and, occasionally, curtailed careers.

• *Concentrate on what you* can *do.* Many of the women I talk to worry that they won't get ahead at work because they can't stay late. I point out that because their children are off to school early, they can put in the extra time in the morning.

Once they stopped dwelling on what was impossible, they were able to channel those energies toward working on a positive solution.

• *Don't be too grateful.* One woman I know thinks that no other man would have married her if her husband had not. Her attitude allows him to take advantage of her. Worse still, he now shares her low opinion of herself and criticizes her frequently.

Another example of this self-defeating behavior is the woman who receives a long-overdue raise and falls all over herself thanking her boss. Express your appreciation, but remember, and remind your boss, that your work justifies that raise—and probably more.

• *Allow yourself to get angry.* Angry feelings are impossible to escape. Burying such feelings usually results in one of two typical outcomes: Either you'll harbor these feelings until you feel depressed, or you'll save them up until you explode in a fit of temper.

Temper tantrums are appropriate for two-year-olds who *are* powerless and helpless. But they are a terrible tactic for grown women. An outburst of temper is regarded as irrational behavior and can easily be dismissed with an "Oh, she must be having a bad day," or, "I guess she got her period." This may leave you feeling even less effectual and subsequently worse than before your outburst.

A more effective technique for dealing with situations that make you angry is to describe them in a single, simple three-part sentence. In the first part, tell the person exactly what the situation is. Second, indicate how that situation makes you feel. Third, present the consequences of those feelings in such a way that the other person sees the payoff or penalty for himself. For example, you might say to your husband: "When you shoot me those warning glances when we're out with your co-workers, I feel afraid to say anything and that makes me reluctant to go at all."

• *Go after the goodies.* You're about to apply for a higher-level position but then tell yourself, "I haven't done anything like that before." Apply anyway. Any new job *should* be a challenge. You aren't expected to know how to do it all the very first day.

• *Try not to settle for less than you should.* Many women believe deep down that they don't deserve the good things in life. Others hold themselves back or make excuses for missing out on advancement opportunities. Some think that any misfortunes that occur are "payment" for the good things that went before. All of these thoughts are part of the syndrome called "fear of success."

These attitudes perpetuate the notion that you are somehow less of a person than you really are. The first step, then, toward becomeing a self-satisfied, successful person is to change your negative perceptions of yourself. Give yourself credit for your accomplishments. Learn to appreciate yourself. After all, you're worth it.

39 | MANAGING FOR THE FUTURE - NOW

ooking into the future is an important tool for business in general and for managers in particular. Projecting from current trends or extrapolating from known data can tell producers what tomorrow will require. For instance, just knowing the number of babies born in 1980 helps pinpoint the 1985 markets for training elementary school teachers, manufacturing children's clothing, selling classroom furniture, building schools, advertising day camps or inventing toys.

Professional Seers

Institutional involvement in futuristics began in this country around the time of World War II, when military concerns about security and defense led to the formation of one of the first "think tanks," the Rand Corporation.

Business has been a little slower to catch on. Surprisingly, futurists place much of the blame for this on their image as "doom and gloomers" ranting about robots, which made them easy to dismiss as "kooks." And, of course, their use of jargon created some communications problems.

Other obstacles emerged from the interaction between futurism and business: Their respective interests were frequently in collision rather than in congruence. James B. Webber, a Lexington, Massachusetts, management consultant, concedes that futurists are far more likely to be fascinated with trends on an intellectual level rather than on a practical one. Arnold Brown, president of Weiner, Edrich, Brown, Inc., a Manhattan consulting firm, considers the substance of futurism threatening.

"Information about change," he says, "is almost always received negatively."

Other critics place the blame on industry itself, pointing out that it can be narrow in its thinking. As Edward S. Cornish, president of the World Future Society and author of its 1977 publication, *The Study of the Future,* observes, "The time perspective of organizational leaders often is startlingly short, generally no more than a year and often less. One futurist who was trying to convince a businessman of the need to think in long-range terms thought he was making progress until the businessman said, 'Yes, I think you are right. We should take time occasionally to think beyond the next quarter.' "

As a consequence, crises have been exacerbated and opportunities overlooked, as in the current situation of the American automobile industry. Cornish continues, "Lack of foresight among organizations has contributed heavily to their failure to deliver the goods and services that their clients expect from them—and often to the collapse of the organizations themselves. . . . The failure of business corporations to see the possibilities in new technology is legendary . . . In 1876 the inventor of the telephone, Alexander Graham Bell, offered exclusive rights to the new invention to Western Union, then the largest communications network in the United States. WU president William Orton was unimpressed. 'What use could this company make of an electrical toy?' "

How Futurists Work

David Pearce Snyder, an independent consultant and author in Bethesda, Maryland, outlines the most commonly used techniques:

Trend extrapolations. Projections based on recent trends. Extrapolating the number of elementary-school students from the number of births could have predicted both the shortage of schoolrooms in the early '60s and the surplus of the late '70s.

Surveys. Collected by using structured interviews or the Delphi technique, a method of soliciting and aggregating individual opinions to arrive at a consensus.

Modeling. Mathematic representations of behavior. An application of modeling would be the number of traffic lanes that should be open in each direction during rush hour.

Scenarios. Descriptions of alternative possible developments. This technique emphasizes that the future is not fixed—not necessarily an extension of the present—nor necessarily bright.

Goal setting. Identifications of the ideal. Goal setting, says Snyder, ignores the present and concentrates on the world we want.

Business Uses Of Futurism

Cornish's book includes the following case histories:

"Back in the 1960s, the Northern States Power Company found itself in the unenviable position of being viewed as public enemy No. 1 by many of the people it served. The Minneapolis-based company was embroiled in costly, head-on battles with environmentalists...(who)...repeatedly succeeded in blocking company plans...NSP's top management sensed that the company's problem was not just the environmentalists, but rather its own reactive decision-making process. ...(They) decided that their first task was to learn about the future, and arranged for teams of NSP employees to interview more than 20 leading futurists....

"Until 1973 the Shell Oil Company each year developed an energy forecast for planning purposes. The forecast was a 10-year analysis of energy supply and demand using the best economic, demographic and political premises available. The single forecast worked well during most of the 1960s but came under question as predictability decayed in the early 1970s... (in 1973)...the company abandoned the old energy forecast entirely and instead provided three scenarios..."

In-house attention to futurism is on the increase. Future-oriented projects have been undertaken at corporations including General Electric, TRW, Bethlehem Steel and Uniroyal, and a few companies have employed full-time futurists. Future-oriented projects may be based in any one of a number of departments: research and development, planning, marketing, human resources (formerly, personnel) or public affairs (formerly, public relations).

Many companies regard at least one of their task forces, committees or departments as a mini-think tank. Think of all the corporations and trade associations that have sponsored conventions, conferences, sales meetings or executive briefings that had "Entering the '80s" as a theme.

Other approaches include:

• *Inviting a futurist to sit on the board.* Edith Weiner was made a director of a life insurance company, a move that her partner, Arnold Brown, terms "quite unusual, but an indicator of things to come."

• *Calling in a consultant.* Ruth Gonchar, former executive vice-president of The Strategy Workshop in New York, says, "Anytime we talk about the way people are changing, *that* information becomes useful to clients. We're pitching the business of a large retailer. That retailer is perfectly aware that fifty-three percent of women work, but the implications of this are passing him by. For instance, only recently he instituted a mail-order catalog."

• *Conducting an environmental scan.* This can be done internally or with the assistance of a consultant.

• *Subscribing to abstracting services.* For example, SRI International in Menlo Park, California, monitors selected publications relating to consumers' values and lifestyles.

What You Can Do

Here are a few guidelines:

• *Learn what is going on in your organization.* Try to get involved.

• *Incorporate a futures perspective into everything.* Consider, for example, the costs and availability of new equipment in calculating your need for clerical personnel. Examine population patterns to determine the location of your new plant. This kind of thinking should influence every decision-maker and not just those charged with long-range planning.

• *Investigate readily available government statistics* before investing in costly consulting services.

• *Overcome managerial myopia.* Think about next month, as well as next week. With the year 1985 approaching and the year 2000 not too far away, it is time to turn from reacting to yesterday's problems and dealing with today's to working on tomorrow's opportunities.

40 | CAREER PATHS

Companies long have had the pieces for career-planning programs—from tuition refunds to training—but only recently have they put the puzzle together. Now large employers from coast to coast—Bank of America, Bank of New York, Detroit Edison, Consolidated Edison, and even some smaller ones—are coordinating their efforts into comprehensive career planning programs for their employees. The beauty of these programs is that, when they are done well, both sides benefit. Beyond such benefits as salary hikes for individual employees, California's Crocker National Bank saved $2 million one year in reduced turnover, improved performance, and increased promotability of staff members who participated in the career-planning program.

Authors Peter Brill, M.D., and John Hayes explain that career development means more than just changing jobs. "It is," they write, "an ongoing process that evaluates abilities and interests, considers alternatives and opportunities, establishes career goals, and plans practical, developmental activities."

The current need to concentrate on career development within a company stems from two separate but simultaneous social forces. First, the notion that there exists only one predestined career per individual has disappeared. Can you imagine anyone asking Donna Shalala, Ph.D., "Can't you hold a job?" when she left the Federal Department of Housing and Urban Development for Hunter College, or someone saying to Lynn Salvage, "Why don't you make up your mind?" when she went from The First Women's Bank in New York to Katharine Gibbs?

Second, there is the "slowdown showdown": With the baby boom generation swelling the ranks of jobholders, the raised retirement age and a slow economy, there are fewer job changes for everyone.

Typical Programs

Marilyn A. Morgan, Ph.D., assistant professor at the University of Pennsylvania's Wharton School, and her colleagues say common components of career development programs are: career counseling; organizational human resources planning; individual career planning; career information systems (including reference libraries, job posting procedures); training and development.

Most corporate programs began as small efforts directed toward specific groups—women, minorities, third-level managers, production supervisors—according to Thomas Gutteridge, Ph.D., associate dean and associate professor at the State University of New York at Buffalo's School of Management. Usually they were started in response to employee interest, Equal Employment Opportunity Commission concerns, or a shortage of home-grown managerial talent. These programs, Gutteridge explains (he has co-authored studies of career-development programs for both the American Society for Training and Development and the American Management Associations), represent an allocation of organizational resources to what is fundamentally seen as an individual responsibility.

Some corporations emphasize the structure and needs of the organization in their programs. Brecker & Merryman, a consulting firm with offices in New York and Los Angeles, which sets up corporate-development programs, uses an eight-step system consisting of work analysis, path development and the creation of paths for each position, which are similar to organizational and personnel flow charts. Andrew Merryman, executive vice-president, criticizes more personalized approaches as liable to raise expectations when "expectations are (already) running too high." He doesn't believe in workbooks and workshops that ask people to fantasize, for instance, about what they would do for a year if money were no obstacle. Such "feel-good exercises," says Merryman, "turn out to have feel-bad results."

Career Management Associates, a New York-based consulting firm, does concentrate on personal rather than organizational planning. It offers exercises to clarify values, identify skills and polish self-presentation. "We teach people to manage their own careers and to maneuver within the organization," explains Richard McCollum, vice-president.

Blessing-White, a Princeton, New Jersey-based consulting firm, emphasizes neither paths nor plans, but postures that permit you to recognize, create and seize opportunities as they arise. Buck Blessing, principal, suggests that a career need not follow a neat road map—much less a Triptik from AAA—but may meander along a "gradual and episodic" route.

Comprehensive Planning

McGraw-Hill, the Manhattan-based publishers (from textbooks to *Business Week* magazine), integrates all of these approaches to career development. Career-planning techniques are related to one another and to other corporate functions as well. Success stories ("I got my job through...") are frequently featured in the house organ to encourage other employees to avail themselves of the services. Employees serve as experts for fellow employees through information interviews as well as through informal lunchtime panel discussions. Company recruiting literature is written from a career planning perspective; it describes both entry-level positions and logical next steps in detail. Succession planning is important, too. Joan Muessen, vice-president, personnel relations administration, explains, "We want to make sure that we have a ready pool for our needs five to ten years in the future and that employees have a place to grow without having to go."

McGraw-Hill's program epitomizes the steps any company should take in installing a career planning system: (1) Involve senior management. Their commitment is essential to the success of any innovation. Their participation signals that such strategies are not restricted to low-level personnel. (2) Tolerate some transfers and terminations. Not all turnover is undesirable. If a poor performer really wants to be a sculptor, you're not losing much if she decides to leave. (3) Utilize both immediate supervisors and staff specialists. Every performance appraisal should include a section on suggested development to foster some discussion of same. (4) Concentrate on developments in place and not just on promotions. (5) Integrate other functions: replacement planning, training and development. You can't develop careers in a vacuum. (6) Communicate what you coordinate or create. What good is it if no one knows about it? (7) Evaluate effectiveness. But be prepared to wait at least three years; don't try to take the program's temperature tomorrow.

Is career planning the career for you? It can be hard to get career-development specialists to talk about their own careers; they have not always followed the sort of planning paths they recommend for others. Buck Blessing of Blessing-White was a tool-and-die maker for ten years before going to college, joining one consulting firm and then founding another. He's the first to concede, "No career path in the world would have gotten me here!"

41 | LEAVING A JOB

O ne of the trickiest—and least discussed—job situations occurs after you decide to leave your job. Even though you have landed your next position, you'll probably have to continue in your current job for at least two weeks, tying up loose ends and smoothing the way for your successor. Psychologists and psychiatrists say it's unlikely that you'll be able to leave any job, even one you disliked, without some anxiety. "Most people—much less organizations—don't have a good way of handling the transition," observes H.G. Whittington, M.D., who has a private practice in psychiatry and behavioral medicine in Denver, Colorado. Your boss may regard your departure as a personal rejection. Your nemesis down the hall suddenly may be nice to you now that you are about to go, and that may make the separation all the harder, Whittington explains. Co-workers' feelings aside, *you* may feel like a lame-duck President—you may hesitate to launch projects or hire staff when you know you won't be there to oversee them.

When you decide to leave your job, you should tell your immediate supervisor first. Then you should tell the people who report to you, because they will be affected most by your departure. Next, tell staff above your boss of your plans, either in person or in writing, depending on the amount of personal contact you have had with them. Last, tell your peers, colleagues and clients.

Bowing Out

Once you've announced your plans, you must try to keep functioning as though you are going to be on the job indefinitely, advises Mortimer R. Feinberg, Ph.D., chairman of the board of BFS Psychological Associates, a management-consulting firm in New York. But following Feinberg's advice is harder than it sounds. There is a great temptation to wind down when you are even thinking about leaving, acknowledges Davia B. Temin, who left her post as director of public affairs for Columbia University's Graduate School of Business to become vice-president and director of marketing for the U.S. division of Citicorp's Capital Markets Group (in New York), earlier this year. Temin tried hard to plan ahead for her public-affairs department, reasoning that Columbia still would be there long after she had left.

Temin made special efforts to assure her superiors, her subordinates and her outside contacts that the transition would be a smooth one. She even discussed the choice of her successor with the dean of the business school, a practice that not every management observer endorses. Whittington, for example, says that wise corporations will not let managers choose their suc-cessors. It requires "superhuman" capacities for a manager to put someone better than herself in her old position for fear of how she will look in comparison. As a result, he says, managers are likely to choose someone who is not quite as good as they are, and the company will suffer.

Whether or not you get involved in hiring your replace-ment, you must ensure that a subordinate will be useful in the interim until your successor is chosen. Have the subordinate sit in on the start-up meetings of any new project so that she or he will be familiar with it when you depart, advises Feinberg. Of course, this well-intended plan can backfire if your acting replacement is so offended when the position is offered to someone else that she or he decides to move on. Obviously, you should not make any promises that you will not be around to guarantee.

The reactions of your co-workers will vary. Your decision to leave implies that there is something better outside your own organization. Your move may prompt co-workers to re-examine their own situations and think about leaving themselves. "The one who leaves is always a renegade and unsettles everyone else," remarks Harriet Rubin, who left her editorial position with Addison-Wesley Publishing Co., Inc., late last year to become an editor at Harper & Row Publishers, Inc. in New York.

One of the ways to lessen tension with co-workers is to down-play your glee about going and to speak of mixed feelings. Temin was circumspect about her feelings with both co-workers and professional connections. She began a letter informing outside associates of her move, "I am both quite pleased and quite saddened to let you know that I will be leaving Columbia Business School. . ."

Even if you have no fond feelings for the employer you are leaving, it pays to put a positive face on things, both because you want to make sure your old employer gives you a good reference and because you never know when you might run into your former co-workers or clients. "Good relations with your ex-employer are a good idea, no matter how bad the experience has been," states Katherine Klotzburger, Ph.D., president of Change-Agents, Inc., a Brooklyn, New York, firm that offers seminars for people leaving their jobs.

Another way to lessen the difficult relations with the co-workers you're leaving is to make the lame-duck period as brief as possible by giving no more notice than you must. Klotzburger finds that male managers fantasize about giving notice at 5:00 p.m. on their last day, while women want to announce their departure weeks, even months, in advance. Women worry about not finishing up work, as a way of masking their anxiety about making the change, Klotzburger surmises. A woman's desire to let people know far in advance also may spring from her delusion of indispensability. Such women are hurt when they learn that personnel can fill their spots in one day or, worse still, that their departments are going to be reorganized and their positions will not be filled at all after they leave.

The wisest course lies in the middle. Giving only one day's notice is irresponsible, but two months' notice is unnecessary. The standard rule—two weeks—probably makes the best sense for most managers.

Trade Secrets

The questions about whom and when to tell seem easy in comparison to those regarding whom and what to take. Can you approach valued clients or customers after you move to a new company, or will that leave you open to charges that you are stealing customers? What about loyal customers who approach you after your move to a new company? You may not be able to do business with them if you signed a contract at your former job, promising not to compete in your old territory. If you designed a new product, can you bring your notes and plans with you? And what about projects that you've developed and presented to your former employer but which your employer has not used by the time you quite to accept a new job?

The answers to these questions aren't clear-cut, unfortunately. Restrictions vary from state to state, and so the problem is a "very touchy subject" that presents a "balancing test for the courts," according to the managing partner of a respected New York law firm. The laws in many states are vague, and so courts decide such matters on a case-by-case basis, the lawyer explains.

Because the law is so fluid, it is difficult to give general guidelines. It may be a good idea to consult a lawyer if you have access to sensitive information or if you have questions about whether the information you bring to your new job belongs to you or to your former employer. This is particularly true if you signed an employment contract with your former employer or if your new company has asked you to sign one.

An area many managers—and companies—know little about is trade secrets. The term refers to anything that is not known generally in your industry, that is kept secret within your company and that gives your company a competitive advantage. Much of the information a manager may possess— methods, formulas, plans, market-research findings, customer lists, and pricing data, for example—may fall under this definition. "While the law imposes an implied duty on employees not to use or disclose their employer's and former employer's trade secrets, most enterprises expressly state that duty in a contract," says Roger M. Milgrim, a noted expert on trade secrets and patents, writing in the *Harvard Business Review*.

The cost to you and your new company of obtaining trade secrets by hiring you can run into millions of dollars if your previous employer files lawsuits that are successful, explains Milgrim. Yet there are unscrupulous employers who are willing to take this risk. One woman once told me about hiring people who had evaluated and selected sites for major corporations. By learning these corporations' growth plans and site criteria, the developer anticipated making advantageous acquisitions of land to convert to industrial parks.

As an employee, you may not even be aware that your new employer is more interested in your inside information about the competition than in your other professional qualities. That your new employer may be buying your inside knowledge may never be discussed outright, says Eleanor Disston Raynolds, vice-president in the New York office of Boyden Associates, Inc., an executive-search firm. "But that's why companies are always asking us to find somebody from another Fortune 100 company in the same line of business," Raynolds explains.

So, pay attention to the trade-secret provisions of any employment contract you sign. Before you leave your current job, the personnel department may remind you of the company's restrictions on the use and disclosure of trade secrets.

While it is necessary to be careful about whom you tell and what you take when you change jobs, the cautionary advice in this chapter should not deter you from moving, for the long-term advantages of a smart career move far outweigh the temporary headaches of the transition.

42 | FACTS OF WORKING LIFE

This is not a AAA Triptik, but merely some rules for the road.

1. *You can make a comeback from a career mistake.* Big businesses do it all the time. Twenty years before signing up Michael Jackson for an ad campaign, PepsiCo passed up another musical sensation. "Who?" you ask. The Beatles!

2. *Employers exaggerate.* Whenever someone starts to paint you a particularly rosy picture, be sure to get what psychologists call a "realistic job" preview. Ask to read your job description. Find out what a typical week is like. Learn what happened to the last person who held the job.

3. *Male colleagues may not be completely comfortable with you.* If you are single, separated, divorced or widowed, you may be treated as a peculiar combination of sexual predator and sexual prey.

4. *Ethical conduct counts.* Koreagate, Abscam, Briefingate and Watergate aside.

5. *More schooling does not ensure more pay.* Women need to learn that master's degrees are not "collectibles."

6. *Competence is hard to measure.* When Betty Rollin applied to be an editor at *Vogue*, she was interviewed and hired. Had she been applying for a secretarial job, she is sure she would have had to take a typing test! Competence may not be quite as important, therefore, as you think. Many managers maintain that they are measuring performance when, in fact, they are taking attendance.

7. *Don't be afraid to change jobs.* If you stay in a bad

situation too long, you may find yourself moving from the frying pan into the fire. Many desperate job seekers accept what I call "the silver platter offer" (one they would never consider, except for the fact that it is being handed to them) and wind up worse off than before. Of course, job hunting is a hassle. Books that promise that you can get the job you want in 28 days are misleading. Perhaps you can acquire *Thin Thighs in 30 Days*, but, once you're beyond the entry level, getting a job takes more than a month.

8. *Remember that it is not only nice, but necessary, to talk about money.* You can enjoy both psychic income and the financial kind. They need not be a tradeoff. Write away for a terrific booklet called *Higher Salaries* by Joyce Lain Kennedy. (Send a check for $3.50 to Box 2000 H, Cardiff, CA 92007). Remember the words of the late Dame Rebecca West, "Women ought to understand that in submitting to this swindle of underpayment, they are not only insulting themselves, but doing a deadly injury to the community."

9. *Remember that working with a friend isn't easy.* People think that it will be a snap, but actually it can be harder than working with a stranger. Two sets of rules apply: those from your relationship and those from the work itself. Spell them out carefully.

10. *Keep up your contacts.* Once you're set in a new job, there is a temptation to concentrate on those in your firm, and forget about others outside. You may need a new job in a hurry and contacts can help you get one. Or you may benefit when an outsider sits next to your boss on a commuter train or scheduled plane and says nice things about you.

| FOR FURTHER READING

In addition to the titles mentioned in the text, you might try these:

Applegath, John. *Working Free.* New York: AMACOM, 1982.

Baruch, Grace, Rosaline Barnett, and Caryl Rivers. *Lifeprints.* New York: McGraw-Hill, 1983.

Bird, Caroline. *The Two-Paycheck Marriage.* New York: Pocket Books, 1979.

Brown, Helen Gurley. *Having It All.* New York: The Linden Press, 1982.

Calano, James and Jeff Salzman. *Real World 101.* New York: Warner Books, 1984.

Fisher, Roger and William Ury, *Getting to Yes.* Boston: Houghton Mifflin, 1981.

Friedman, Martha. *Overcoming the Fear of Success.* New York: Seaview Books, 1980.

Half, Robert. *The Robert Half Way to Get Hired in Today's Job Market.* New York: Bantam Books, 1983.

Harragan, Betty Lehan. *Games Mother Never Taught You.* New York: Warner Books, 1977.

Jackson, Tom. *Guerrilla Tactics in the Job Market.* New York: Bantam Books, 1978.

Kanter, Rosabeth Moss. *The Change Masters.* New York: Simon & Schuster, 1983.

Kanter, Rosabeth Moss. *Men and Women of the Corporation.* New York: Basic Books, 1977.

Kleiman, Carol. *Women's Networks.* New York: Ballantine, 1980.

Posner, Mitchell J. *Executive Essentials.* New York: Avon Books, 1982.

Rollin, Betty. *Am I Getting Paid For This?* Boston: Little, Brown, 1982.

Rosenbaum, Bernard L. *How to Motivate Today's Workers.* New York: McGraw-Hill, 1982.

Scheele, Adele M. *Skills for Success.* New York: William Morrow, 1979.

Siegelman, Ellen Y. *Personal Risk.* New York: Harper & Row, 1983.

Whittlesey, Marietta. *Freelance Forever.* New York: Avon Books, 1982.

Winston, Stephanie. *The Organized Executive.* New York: W. W. Norton, 1983.

Wyse, Lois. *The Six-Figure Woman.* New York: The Linden Press, 1983.

HOW YOU CAN GET AHEAD WITH CAREERTRACK

Request your FREE CareerTrack catalog of seminars and tapes...

From communication skills, to self-management, to career success strategies, CareerTrack brings you a message of excellence, productivity, imagination and pride.

Founded in 1982 by Jimmy Calano and Jeff Salzman, CareerTrack is the largest business seminar company in North America. Hundreds of thousands of success-oriented professionals look to CareerTrack for the get-ahead information they need. CareerTrack presents over 2000 seminars a year in more than 350 cities throughout the United States, Canada and Australia. It also offers private programs presented to your people at your convenience. Its sister company, CareerTrack Publications, publishes audio and video tapes on a wide range of self-help and professional-development topics.

For your free catalog of CareerTrack's seminars and tapes, just return the coupon below.

Three Essential Books for the
Professional Woman on the Way Up

___ **REACH YOUR CAREER DREAMS!** $15.95

The Essential Handbook for Professional Women ($22.50, Canada)
by CareerTrack's Highest-Rated Seminar Trainers

Have your own team of expert advisors for making your career dreams come true. From setting realistic goals, to boosting your self-image, to communicating with authority, to networking for advancement — *Reach Your Career Dreams!* — is a powerful, fun-to-read, easy-to-put-into-action handbook that can literally change your life. *(220 pages, hardcover)*

___ **ADVANCED CAREER STRATEGIES FOR WOMEN** $15.95

How to Make It to the Top Faster ($22.50, Canada)
by Marilyn Machlowitz, Ph.D.

This is the career book for women already climbing the success ladder. It's *not* about how to break into the corporate world — but how to make it to the top. In 40 crisp chapters, Machlowitz (the nationally-known career columnist), presents strategies that are working for today's most successful professional women. Topics range from gaining visibility inside and outside your company, to career-pathing, to understanding corporate politics — and much more. *(212 pages, hardcover)*

___ **PERSONAL POWER** $15.95

The Guide to Power for Today's Working Woman ($22.50, Canada)
by Arleen LaBella and Dolores Leach

Are you uncomfortable having to take charge of certain situations? Do people resist or even ignore you when you try to exercise power? With this best-selling book, learn the *attitudes of power:* how to look, think and act like a high-achiever. You'll also gain the *tools of power:* risk-taking, decision-making, power communication, competition and collaboration. *(184 pages, hardcover)*

_____ **IT'S EASY TO ORDER** _____

Please send me the book(s) I've checked.

My method of payment is: Total amount of order $ _____

☐ Check (payable to CareerTrack Publications, Inc.) Check # _____

☐ Please charge to the following credit card:

    ☐ VISA   ☐ MASTERCARD   ☐ AMEX   Exp. Date

Credit Card Number   Month   Year

_____ Cardholder's signature

Please ship to:

NAME _____

ADDRESS _____
    (PLEASE. NO P.O. BOXES.)

CITY _____ STATE _____ ZIP _____

DAY PHONE (_____) _____ EXT. _____

Please allow 3-4 weeks for delivery. Mail payment with order form to:
CareerTrack Publications • 1800 38th Street • Boulder, CO 80301.
Or call (303) 447-2300.

YOUR GUARANTEE: If the products you order are not to your liking, please return them within 15 days. Tell us whether you want a replacement or a full refund and we will get it to you promptly.

— CLIP OR PHOTOCOPY —

From CareerTrack's Founders . . .
Two "Must-Read" Books to Move Your Career Further, Faster